The Four Secret Rings of Love and Happiness

Discover the keys that open the secret to self-love, intimacy, communication, common goals and values in your relationship and, most of all, with yourself!

Richard Henry II Hains, CD, BAp, MSc, MBA, EMBA
Couple & Relationship Psychotherapist

Copyright 2016 by Richard Henry II Hains

All rights reserved. No part of this book may be reproduced in any form without permission in writing from the publisher, except in the case of brief quotations embodied in critical articles or reviews.

While the author and publisher used their best efforts in preparing this book, they make no representations or warranties with respect to the accuracy or completeness of the contents of this book. The advice and strategies contained herein may not be suitable for your situation. You should consult with a professional where appropriate. Neither the author nor publisher shall be liable for any loss of profit or any other commercial and personal damages, including but not limited to special, incidental, consequential, or other damages.

Library of Congress Cataloging-in-Publication Data
Richard Henry II Hains

The Four Secret Rings of Love and Happiness / Richard Henry II Hains

ISBN-13: 978-0-9986806-2-0

1. Marriage 2.Communication in marriage. 3. Love. I. Title.

We hope you enjoy this book from French Amour. Our goal is to provide high quality, thought provoking books and products that connect truth to your real needs and challenges.

to Henry, Rose, and Andrea

The Four Secret Rings of Love and Happiness

The Four Secret Rings of Love and Happiness

is a trademark of

Other Books by French Amour,

The Journal - The Four Secret Rings™

A Date in Paris - The Online Dating Cleansing Program™

The Secret Art of French Love-Making™ (coming soon)

Golden Heart™ (coming soon)

Contents

Acknowledgement
1. Introduction..15
2. The First Secret Ring: Self-Love...................21
3. The Second Secret Ring: Intimacy................55
4. The Third Secret Ring: Communication....113
5. The Fourth Secret Ring: Common Goals
   and Values..159
6. Gabrielle's Journey......................................197
7. Conclusion..223

Acknowledgement

The life of an author is filled with blessings, courage, and wisdom. A book is never written alone. People and the environment surrounding you bring inspiration and the motivation to complete this labor of love.

In this particular case, our Creator is the first one to be thankful to. He is the source of eternal love between one another. He is the one who ultimately inspired me to write this book. Working for Him, in so many ways, to spread love and happiness in relationships is a true blessing.

Then, my grandparents, Henry and Rose Hains, are my absolute second. They took me under their protection when I was just a child, and with an enormous amount of patience, guidance, and love, they made me the man I am today. I owe them my current blessings. Thank you, Gran-Pa and Gran-Ma.

My wife and children are my everything. Andrea, the woman with the golden heart, is my very best friend, my confidant, my amazing lover, and my ultimate partner traveling this journey called life. She shares and lives, on a daily basis, the principles and secrets revealed in this book. Our children Jonathan, Emily, Lauren, and Jaxon are also my source of love and inspiration. It warms our hearts to think that, as parents, we are making a difference in their lives. Friends and family have been a tremendous support, believing in me and encouraging the pursuit in revealing this book.

Introduction

Love and Relationships the Way You always Wanted

Love and happiness in a relationship seem elusive, and yet we are all constantly in search of their power. Being happy and in love with someone is one of the most rewarding human experiences one can ever enjoy. God created us as equal parts seeking a perfect counter-balance in our soul mate.
However, after we pass the euphoric stage, we need to find out what creates the foundation of a long-lasting healthy relationship. This book is in your hands to guide you to that answer. Everything happens for a reason, and you are reading these words in order to uncover these secrets.

Have you ever wondered?

- Why are happiness and love in a relationship so elusive?
- Why do most marriages fail?
- Why do you find yourself empty and generally unhappy in a relationship?
- Why do partners grow apart never knowing why?
- Why do you not feel understood or cared about when you are trying to communicate?
- Why do intimacy and sex feel empty?
- Why is your relationship not nourishing your soul the way it should?

Why do you simply feel unhappy?

Did you ever think that perhaps there are certain elements, principles, or fundamentals that guarantee a happy and fulfilling relationship with your partner? Did you ever wonder if there were principles that guarantee the nourishment of your soul?

If I were to tell you the fundamentals of love and happiness or, more precisely, the most important attributes of a healthy relationship, what would you do? What would you really do?

Would you invest the time to learn these life-changing skills to ensure your happiness?

The Four Secret Rings of Love and Happiness takes a different approach from anything you have been exposed to before.

The Four Secret Rings of Love and Happiness solves this eternal problem. It will teach you how to live with love and happiness in your relationship and, more importantly, it will teach you how to live these principles within yourself.

I've combined the fascinating aspects of the French culture with the power of over two decades of clinical research in the field of couples and relationship therapy to give you the Four Secrets of Love and Happiness. In this beautiful story, which takes place in the south of France, you will meet

Émilie Durant and follow her journey as she discovers the Four Secret Rings of Love and Happiness. Along the way, she will reveal the secret power of Love and Happiness.

Her story will become your story. Her journey will become your journey. Everyone seeking love and happiness in a relationship will learn the following critical skills:

- How to love yourself for who you are, and feel complete and at peace.
- How to develop and live out an amazing sex life with your partner.
- How to develop healthy communication skills where both partners feel understood and cherished.
- Finally, discover the foundations for success in your relationship with shared and agreed-upon common goals and values.

As a trained couples and relationship psychotherapist, I've studied and researched the principles of love and happiness for decades. I have spent countless hours studying, practicing, and teaching the key fundamentals for success in any relationship.

Love and happiness did not exist in the earlier part of my childhood. This is a large part of the reason why I developed an interest in, and passion for, healthy relationships. I grew up in a broken home where I experienced daily abuse and violent behavior at the hands of my father. My brothers and mother also suffered the same daily treatment. I was kidnapped, along with my brothers, at the age of ten and kept away from my family for over a year. A year after our return, my mother abandoned my brothers and me, never to reach out or contact any of us again.

However, my grandparents took me in and raised me like their own son. They fixed the "broken wings" given to me by a decade of great abuse. They showed me, with immense patience, the way to love, happiness in a healthy relationship. Their love gave me the courage and passion to research and practice the fundamental components of any healthy relationship.

Émilie's story can be anyone's story. Émilie's journey can be everyone's journey. This passionate and life transforming adventure is unique. It will guide you to the four secret rings that Émilie Durant discovered and acquired while collecting the knowledge necessary to be happy and in love in her relationships and, most of all, with herself.

As she discovers the secrets of love and happiness, you will also be transformed into a new version of yourself.

You will learn the secrets of...

- Self-Love. By far the most valuable secret, it will set the tone of any healthy relationship.

- Amazing tantric intimacy.

- The power of healthy communication.

- The grounding foundation of common values and goals in your relationship.

<u>I promise one thing and one thing only.</u> With the four secret rings of love and happiness applied to your life, your feelings of anguish, sadness, and melancholy will be transformed. You will never feel the same again. A sense of empowerment, control over your destiny, and of love for yourself and your partner will surge.

Why live another day without the secrets to love and happiness? Why wait another minute? You have the power to change your life, and live in a loving and happy relationship right now! Why wait and feel more pain and misery? Never feel victimized again. Follow Émilie's journey and you, too, will be transformed.

Follow Émilie's journey and learn from her experiences, and I PROMISE YOU that you, too, will have a relationship that you always dreamed of, filled with love and happiness.

You have the power <u>RIGHT NOW</u> to change your relationship and yourself forever. <u>YOU</u> have the power in your hands to learn and apply the principles of self-love. You have the power to learn and put into practice the amazing effect of great intimacy tonight. Apply your communication skills and gain a mutual understanding with your partner today. Develop, with your loved one, common goals and values that will form the bedrock of a powerful bond.

Empower yourself **NOW!**

The First Secret Ring

Self-Love and the Art of Completeness

The journey to The Four Secret Rings of Love and Happiness always starts with oneself. Always! This concept is critical to understand if you are to cultivate a healthy and loving relationship. It is virtually impossible to be truly happy and love someone in a healthy relationship if self-love is not present and well.

This first secret represents the soil in which all other aspects of a healthy relationship take root.

It is interesting to notice that, culturally, the French are more inclined to cultivate healthy self-love. Just from a self-appreciation perspective, it is easy to understand that French people pay close attention to their self-image. This characteristic of the culture has been dominant for thousands of years. This self-image, in return, has a profound impact on one's self-esteem and, ultimately, one's feeling of self-worth.

ଔ

Émilie's journey to The Four Secret Rings of Love and Happiness starts early in the spring of 1944 in the south of France. The area represents everything that makes France so charming. The region of St. Girons is bordered by valleys, rivers, and lush grazing pastures. It's a picture postcard setting. Since March of that year, the climate had been perfect. The seemingly never-ending sunshine and even temperatures made the *vignerons* (wine makers) joyous and happy. The general atmosphere was as if the little community was oblivious to the traumatic events of World War II that were occurring in Paris and the surrounding areas.

Michelle Durant, Émilie's mother, was an avid gardener. She had been gardening since she was a child. Michelle regularly received compliments about how beautiful her garden looked. She prided herself in growing all the varieties of roses available in France. Her garden also boasted a wide array of fruits and vegetables. Each day, Michelle collected some of the ripe produce for the family *souper* (supper). Émilie and her father Ernest could never believe how perfect the vegetables and fruits were. Whenever she received a compliment about her garden, Michelle would touch her silver ring and say, "*Merci!*" Sometimes she would add that she was simply applying the secrets she received from her mother when she was a young girl. Family and friends often asked how she managed to grow such a bountiful garden. Michelle would always reply, "*l'amour de soi*" (self-love), but no one seemed to understand how the concept related to fruit, vegetables, or flowers.

Émilie's journey to the Four Secret Rings of Love and Happiness started with a breakthrough. She had been extremely upset with her recent *rupture* (breakup). Her latest heartbreak stemmed from a failed relationship with Stéphane, the mayor's oldest son. They had only been seeing each other for a few months when it ended. Stéphane was polite and well mannered, as well as very thoughtful and respectful toward Émilie, although he was not always the most romantic. Their relationship had been *tumultuse* (rocky) from the beginning.

Émilie never had a problem getting male attention. She was extremely beautiful with her long blond curly hair, bright blue eyes, and slender and toned physique. She was high-spirited and had an ill self-love. At times, her mindset did not match her stunning beauty. Her vision of love and self-love was misguided... to say the least.

Émilie really liked Stéphane. He was from a good family and had a brilliant future ahead of him. He also had a healthy image of himself and did not take the way Émilie treated him very well. As for Émilie, her sadness didn't come from the breakup, but rather from her disappointment with her own relationship abilities. Something was missing, or rather, something was lacking in her ability to maintain a healthy relationship with herself—or anyone else for that matter.

Michelle was saddened to see her daughter in such a state. At the same time, Michelle was irritated by her continuous, destructive pattern of failed and unhappy relationships. She always seemed to go straight from the honeymoon phase to the "let down". Inevitably, she finished all of her liaisons with a *volée* of disastrous communication mishaps and a poor showing of character. Émilie needed help!

That day, Émilie hit rock bottom. Crying and screaming in her bedroom, she buried her head deep in her pillow and tried to chase the pain away. Michelle sat by Émilie's bedside, gently caressing her hair, trying to calm her down. Soon her uncontrollable sobbing stopped, and she allowed herself to relax and be comforted by the nurturing touch of her mother. Seizing the opportunity to help Émilie learn something valuable, Michelle whispered into her daughter's ear,

"Tu dois apprendre à t'aimer avant de pouvoir aimer quelqu'un d'autre." ("You must learn to love yourself first before you can truly love someone else.")

Émilie raised her head from the pillow and looked at her mother.

"Why do I suffer in all my relationships?" she asked bitterly.

Michelle repeated, "Émilie, you must learn how to love yourself before you can be happy and loved in a relationship. It's that simple."

Émilie did not understand, although it was not the first time she had heard this from her mother.

However, this time, she heard it a little differently. The emotional growing pains Émilie had endured over the past few years had to stop. She was ready to start her journey on the path to the French *art de l'amour*.

༄*French Secret*༄

The French art de l'amour is also another way to characterize The Four Secret Rings to Love and Happiness.

"Tell me about self-love, *Maman*. Tell me what I need to do!" Émilie begged in desperation.

"Your grandmother Nanny Violet taught me this principle when I was about your age," her mother explained. "She taught me to be my own best friend first."

Émilie was intrigued by the concept of self-love, but becoming her own best friend was a lot to grasp for her.

"What are the principles of self-love?" Émilie asked as she reached into her bedside table to retrieve a notebook. "What does being 'your own best friend' mean?"

Michelle smiled. Her daughter was ready. She could see it in her eyes. Émilie was smart and determined by nature. Her journey had begun.

Michelle took Émilie's hand, "Are you really ready for this fantastic journey?" she asked.

Émilie nodded.

"I am glad to see that you took your notebook out. This 'vessel' will transport you to higher ground. My journal was instrumental in my own personal growth," Michelle said, reflecting.

ꙮFrench Secretꙮ

French people love journaling! It is not unusual to find best friends reading passages from their journals to one another while sipping a café au lait at a bistro. The act of sharing one's most intimate secrets and innermost thoughts strengthens the relationship and also invites personal breakthroughs.

Émilie sat straight up in bed and focused on her mother's every word. Michelle took a deep breath, closed her eyes, and started to explain the five principles of self-love. "The first step on your journey to the French *art de l'amour* is finding the ability to assume complete responsibility for your actions and the outcomes they create. Being response-ABLE means the ability to choose the response that benefits you, a response that enables you to grow. It gives you control over your life and prevents you from feeling victimized by your environment. Every time you use excuses or blame someone else for your current situation, you lose an opportunity to better your life. You lose the chance to take another step along your journey."

Émilie frantically wrote every word down. When she completed the last sentence she looked up and said, "I love you," to her mother.

Michelle reached over and gave her a grateful kiss. "I love you too, my dear. You will feel so much better when you start applying all of the principles you are about to learn. Are you ready for the second principle?" Michelle prodded.

"Yes, of course, *Maman*," Émilie replied.

Michelle looked at Émilie. "The second step or principle is the ability to recognize the blessings that are showered upon you. Each day you must take some time, preferably in the morning, to remind yourself of at least five beautiful qualities, achievements, or blessings in your life. The more you focus on what you are grateful for, the more you will attract the same into your life. This focus will also help increase your sense of self-worth," Michelle explained.

Émilie was puzzled. "Self-worth. What does that mean, *Maman*?"

Michelle smiled. Her inquisitive mind was a sign that Émilie would make progress quickly. "I am glad you asked, Émilie. Self-worth is simply how you value yourself. It's how you feel about your innermost soul. The more you see yourself with esteem, the more doors will open along your journey," she said.

Émilie still had her puzzled look. "I'm not sure if I understand that concept right now, and I'm certain I don't appreciate its full meaning. Perhaps we could talk some more after afternoon tea?" Her face brightened, and she grinned.

Michelle took her daughter by the hand. Without saying a word, they went downstairs, gathered up their gardening tools, and went to tend the garden.

Émilie did not say much that afternoon. She was reflective and wasn't paying much attention to her gardening. Her mother's words were too consuming. She still had so many questions that needed to be answered. It was the first taste of what was to come into her life.

Michelle prepared tea later in the afternoon, after they had had some quiet time in the garden. When she went to the house to boil the water for their daily ritual, Émilie scurried off and retrieved the notebook from her bedroom. It had been some time since she had written anything in it. The little book was mostly filled with sad, disjointed entries. She had begun to feel that she owed it to herself to grow. What was more, she realized that she needed to start to take responsibility for her actions. This notebook was to become the first of many testaments along her journey. As they sat down for tea, Michelle noticed something different in Émilie's smile. It wasn't her ordinary smile. It was a smile of enlightenment.

"I see that you've started your journey. I remember my first day, too. I had an incredible lifting emotion come over me," Michelle described as she raised her hands towards the sky.

"Yes. I feel that. Something is changing, *Maman*." Émilie nodded.

"Then let's continue, shall we?" her mother suggested. "You know, Émilie, no one is perfect but we must strive to improve the little wrinkles that we hold in ourselves. One wrinkle at the time, you must be able to work on yourself to try to improve. This is the third principal of self-improvement. The fourth is about forgiveness.

Émilie interrupted her mother. "I think forgiveness will be difficult for me. I can never seem to let go of negative thoughts or things that have been said to me. I often feel resentment and the need for vengeance towards anyone who has hurt me. But when I react that way, I feel guilty and sorry for myself," Émilie admitted, noticeably ashamed.

"Don't worry, my child, we will work on all of that when the time comes," Michelle reassured her.

Émilie's shame lifted somewhat. She smiled and invited her mother to share more. "Are there any other principles that I must follow to be able to love myself completely?" she asked.

"Yes, there is one more. The last principle is the ability to appreciate and nurture your mind, body and soul. We call this principle *self-appreciation*," Michelle answered with a nod.

Émilie did not understand all of the principles of self-love her mother had described. However, the desire to be in love with herself had begun to burn deep within her. Émilie's journey to the French *art de l'amour* was under way.

The following Sunday morning, Michelle sat near her "Garden of Eden", as she called it. She was lost in thought, admiring her precious garden. Every flower, vegetable, and tree was in bloom. It was another beautiful spring day in southern France. Sipping a cup of tea, she heard Émilie coming from the house.

"*Maman, Maman, où es-tu?*" ("Mother, Mother, where are you?")

Michelle replied, "*Je suis ici, mon ange*". ("I am here, angel.")

Émilie approached quickly, then paused and stood for a moment to admire the beautiful garden. "*Maman*! Perhaps I've never taken the time to really admire it before, but I don't think I have ever seen your garden look so beautiful," she observed.

Michelle humbly responded, "I assume full responsibility for the quality of these blooms. Other than the help of God, nothing else made this come true. You see, Émilie, by accepting the fact that I am entirely responsible for the outcome of my life, I have given myself the power to make the appropriate changes when I am not happy with the result. For example, take this small rosebush. Do you remember how it was faltering?" she asked, waving her hand toward the vibrant plant.

"Yes, *Maman*." Émilie nodded.

"If I blamed the temperature or the lack of water, or simply assumed that the reason it wasn't thriving was its own destiny, well... it likely would have died. Instead, I assumed complete responsibility for the outcome and took the appropriate actions. I watered it more and gave it a little bit of fertilizer. Now it's happy and blooming," she said proudly, re-emphasizing her earlier teaching.

ɞFrench Secretɞ

Being response-ABLE is a simple concept and yet it holds the most amazing power. The act of taking full responsibility is empowering. It is VITAL for a healthy relationship and in life in general. When both partners share this power and recognize their part of the current state of the relationship, many common problems stop. Suddenly there is no room for blaming, criticizing, or judging. Instead, the communication is filled with praise and joy.

Émilie could not stop smiling. She felt as if she had just discovered an amazing treasure.

Michelle continued. "You can also apply this principle to your relationship. You see, Émilie, if you are response-able then you can choose the way you ACT rather than REACT. You will be able to choose your responses carefully and create the result you are looking for. Accepting responsibility for your current state will give you the power to change the outcome. Putting this principle into practice will render the use of criticizing, blaming, judging, and emotional flooding useless. These communication sins have no place in a healthy relationship," Michelle elucidated, speaking from experience.

Émilie was bewildered by the amount of wisdom her mother possessed.

Michelle stood up and brushed the dirt off her beautiful red apron. "Come, Émilie. We need to go to the market for tonight's dinner. Our neighbors are coming over for a celebration."

The village of St. Girons was a close-knit community. No one felt alone. Everyone helped one another and gathered together for important events. That night, Jean-Marcel and Claudette Dutois, neighbors who owned a nearby winery, were coming over to celebrate the beginning of the season. Their family had been growing and harvesting cabernet grapes for centuries. The region of St. Girons was known for its temperature stability and soil, but the Dutois' grapes always received particular adulation. The evening was wonderful, full of great food, wine, and conversation. Émilie couldn't help but notice how much she felt at ease. She was happy, and she knew that the lessons she was learning from her mother were the reason.

Several days passed without Michelle and Émilie talking about self-love. However, something remarkable was happening. Émilie was growing from the inside out, from the roots of her soul to the beautiful bloom of her spirit. She had been carrying her notebook with her everywhere she went, taking notes on her breakthroughs and deep introspection. That day, Émilie made some self-affirmations.

Émilie started to see her soul as a beautiful garden. One of her daily priorities had become to always bring out the best in herself. Her routine started each morning. She'd close her eyes and think of five blessings she was grateful for. Whenever she did, a beautiful smile of joy illuminated her face as she recorded these daily blessings in her journal. As she adopted this habit, she began to notice that her days started with happiness and always got better as the day took its course. She began to learn that the more she focused on what she wanted in life, the more it showed up in reality. Émilie had become the product of her thoughts and not of her environment. This was a major breakthrough for her.

The sun shone brightly the next morning in St. Girons. Fresh, moist air drifted down from the mountains, leaving a beautiful carpet of dew over the pastures. Émilie put on her mother's red apron and her *sabots* (wooden shoes). On her way out, she grabbed a large silver bucket that was sitting on a bench near the door. When she arrived at the garden, she took a moment to admire the beauty that was in front of her. As she had done so many times before with her mother, Émilie began removing the weeds that had crept up. However, she had found a new meaning in this practice. While she attended the flower bed, Émilie took time to reflect. Like pulling the weeds, she removed any trace of judgment, negativity, and criticism in her heart, leaving only room for the bright sunlight to enter her spirit and bring out the most ravishing color and bloom of her personality. Émilie was transforming.

࿇*French Secret*࿇

Apply self-affirmation with your family and friends. There is nothing like a sincere compliment to bring sunlight to someone's life.

Michelle and Ernest understood the importance of bringing sunlight into each other's hearts. They loved showering one another with sincere daily compliments. They also looked forward to sharing special moments of affection, which always brought the brightest bloom to their relationship. They shared a glow on their faces that reflected their healthy, thriving, and loving union. In the garden of love, nothing brings out more gratitude than the gentle act of appreciation for one another.

↭*French Secret*↭

Physical affection (such as kisses and caresses) is, for the French, what water is for plants: a source of life.

Michelle knew the secret of a beautiful garden. She applied the third principle of self-love, self-improvement, daily. She knew that even the most perfect plants and flowers would, at some point, need a bit of improvement in order to achieve their full potential. Just like she did in her garden, she focused on the details and always sought out chances to self-improve.

"Nobody's perfect," Michelle would say. "But with the help of God, every day offers me the chance to improve so I can continue my growth to personal blossoming."

Émilie sat beside her mother that morning, admiring the vivid colors of the roses. Their fresh, intoxicating fragrance filled the garden.

"*Maman*, why are your roses so colorful and crisp? They look so perfect!" Émilie praised in admiration.

Michelle looked at her and smiled graciously. "Émilie, are you ready to explore the third principle of self-love further?" she asked, inviting her daughter to learn more.

"Yes, of course. Please tell me more. I'll get my notebook from my bedroom," Émilie replied excitedly. She stood up and ran into the house. A short time later, she returned with her red notebook and two glasses of lemon tea, her mother's favorite.

"Here, *Maman*, I brought your favorite." Émilie beamed.

"You are the best daughter in the entire world, my angel," Michelle replied, touched by the kind gesture. She took her cup of tea and sat beside Émilie. Taking a sip, she cleared her throat and gathered her thoughts. "Self-improvement is the third principle of self-love and is also the secret behind the wonderful color of these roses."

Michelle paused a moment to allow Émilie to catch up in her writing. She continued, "Every living being needs to grow or it will die. I fertilize these roses often to allow them to grow. Without that care, they would never turn out as healthy. Human beings are the same," Michelle explained, pausing for another sip of tea.

"We need fertilizer, too?" Émilie asked.

"Yes, my angel. Our fertilizer, which is different for everyone, is the application of new knowledge. It is also our ability to recognize what our personal areas of self-improvement are. When we take full response-ability and apply new knowledge in our life to grow and bloom, we radiate the most attractive fragrance of our souls," said Michelle, looking at her daughter.

Émilie enjoyed her mother's poetic metaphors and asked, "*Maman*, how can I put this principle into my daily self-love practice?"

Michelle smiled. "That is easy. As you stop for few minutes each day to truly appreciate your blessings, think of only one thing you could do that day to improve. Then, write it down in your journal and think of a few actions that you could take that day to bring you closer to your accomplishment. You see, Émilie, it is not about overwhelming yourself or forcing change, but rather having patience and giving grace to the process of improvement. Practice this daily. Take consistent little steps, and the results will show. This is how we grow, just like the gentle flowers of the garden. If you try to correct them too quickly, they will die. Give them time to acclimatize to their new state, and they will blossom."

Émilie felt a wave of understanding rush over her. She was taken by this very simple yet powerful truth. "I know exactly what I need to improve, *Maman*," Émilie said.

"Tell me, Émilie," asked Michelle, excited to hear her discovery.

"I need to be my own best friend. I need to prove to myself that I can embody the character of an *amitiée durable* (best friend qualities). I need to keep myself honest with my own feelings and not compromise them to please anyone else. I also need to keep my word. I need to be trustworthy and dependable. I must trust in myself and be true to my word. I must also learn to listen and not judge. I am often too quick to respond. I am often not response-able for the outcome I am seeking. I need to take time to really understand what others are saying, rather than assume what they are saying," she announced, feeling enlightened.

Michelle began to cry. Tears of happiness gently flowed down her cheeks. Émilie was embracing the French *art de l'amour*. Her journey to love and happiness was underway.

Michelle had never imagined she would become a spiritual leader for her daughter. The gift of love was by far the most beautiful gift anyone could give. She was overwhelmed with pride.

Émilie became noticeably happier every day. Self-love was purifying her heart and creating the perfect attitude within her for her future love in her life. Becoming her own best friend gave her wings for the journey to the French *art de l'amour*. Her notebook was always by her side. Émilie relished capturing her breakthroughs and "Ah-hah!" moments. It brought her great joy to pull the "bad weeds" from her "Garden of Love". However, as she cleared her soul of negativity, she started to feel ashamed and embarrassed by her past behavior towards herself and others. Émilie was so humiliated by her past actions that she felt like crying. She needed to talk to her mother about these feelings. She wondered if it was normal.

It was just after four in the afternoon when Michelle and Émilie sat in the *petite terrasse* (little patio) outside the house. They admired the sunset and sipped their *pétales de roses* (rose petal) tea. Émilie took out her little red notebook to go over some of her thoughts and breakthroughs with her mother. As she revealed some of her most guarded secrets, Émilie began to cry.

"*Maman*, I am ashamed of some of my behavior," said Émilie with tears in her eyes.

"My poor angel, rest your soul. It is perfectly normal to feel this way. In fact, it's healthy," said Michelle empathetically.

Émilie did not know what to think but she trusted her mother's wisdom.

"It's normal to feel this way as you begin to grow. Journaling gives us the ability to reflect on ourselves. I think it is time to tell you about the fourth principle, self-forgiveness. This principle is one of the most powerful gifts of self-love," Michelle declared.

"Why, *Maman*?" Émilie asked.

"The ability to cleanse your soul, to 'let go' of the bad weeds that occupied your garden, will ensure that your spirit stays vigorous and free of resentment, misfortune, and anger."

Once again, Michelle used her garden as a metaphor to explain the power and beautiful transformation that self-love can bring to one's life.

"Tell me more about forgiveness," Émilie asked, turning to a blank page of her journal.

"Forgiveness doesn't mean that you disregard the other person's responsibility for hurting you. It doesn't minimize or justify the wrong. However, you can still forgive the person without excusing the act. Forgiveness will bring peace to your soul and calmness to your life," Michelle explained. "If you dwell on hurtful events or situations, resentment and thoughts of vengeance will start to take root in your garden." Her mother paused to allow this wonderful truth to sink in with Émilie. "As you let go of grudges, you'll no longer define your life by how you've been hurt, but you will find compassion and understanding for the other person," she said, allowing Émilie to finish taking notes.

Her mother continued as she refilled her daughter's tea. "Getting another person to change their actions, behavior, or words isn't the point of forgiveness. The act of forgiveness changes your life by bringing you peace, happiness, and spiritual healing. Forgiveness takes away the emotional power of the situation."

Émilie eagerly wrote down every word so she could reflect upon it later and fully absorb the truth and power of this wonderful teaching.

"How do we cleanse our souls of bad weeds?" Émilie inquired.

"Well, I do have a routine that I practice every night. Before I go to bed, I remove my silver ring and take time to forgive myself and anyone else who may have hurt me. Doing so gives me a clear conscience and allows me to sleep well."

With that, they looked at each other and felt a deeper understanding emerging between them.

ಏFrench Secretಏ

The power of forgiveness is sacred. It prevents negative emotional energy from creeping up in your Garden of Love.

Several weeks passed without Michelle speaking to her daughter about self-love. Émilie's progress was most impressive. She had become a different person. Like a chrysalis opening to the world, Émilie was becoming a beautiful butterfly. She was light on her feet and happy. Her notebook was filled with breakthroughs, memories, and observations of past events. Émilie had a clear sight as to who she was becoming: a love angel. She enjoyed doing her morning and evening rituals. When she woke up, she would look at her journal and think of five blessings she had received the day before. Then she reminded herself of the actions she needed to take to advance in her self-improvement. In the evening, just before bed, she would close her eyes and allow forgiveness to enter her heart. She imagined removing the "bad weeds" that crept up in her Garden of Love that day. Émilie was also very fond of writing in the morning just after breakfast. She'd take her *café au lait* with her and find a place near her mother's garden where bees, butterflies, and hummingbirds flew about, carefree. Émilie was becoming a source of the love around her. Only one principle remained unearthed in order to complete her journey to self-love, and her spiritual leader, Michelle, was about to reveal it to her.

"I'm so happy with myself lately, *Maman*," Émilie announced to her mother as she prepared to get eggs from their farm.

"Yes, I've noticed, Émilie. You are well underway on your journey to the French *art de l'amour*," Michelle acknowledged with a grin. "When you come back, I will teach you the last principle of self-love. We'll go to the garden with some lemon tea."

"Marvelous," Émilie chimed as she walked out the door into the glorious morning.

Michelle was already tending her garden when Émilie appeared with her journal and a tray of lemon tea.

"I am ready to learn about the last principle of self-love, *Maman*," Émilie announced as she put down the tray.

"Very well, let's have some tea before we start," her mother suggested. Michelle took a long sip of her favorite tea and began.

"The last principle is extremely important, Émilie. Oftentimes, we take who we have become for granted and forget to celebrate ourselves. The last principle is about creating the opportunity to delight in yourself. It is self-appreciation," Michelle noted. "Every day, you need to find ways to appreciate yourself. You need to give joy to your mind, body, and soul. You have to ask yourself, "'What can I do today to make myself happy?'"

As Émilie finished writing the last word, she confessed, "I'm not sure what you mean by giving joy to my mind, body, and soul."

Michelle nodded, "Don't worry, my child. I will explain, and you will understand it perfectly. Every day, I think of things that I could do to bring joy to my mind. For me, I love doing crossword puzzles with *Papa*. It gives me the greatest pleasure. I love to challenge my intellect by trying to find the right word. As you know, I also enjoy reading and memorizing poems," she said, looking at Émilie.

"I see. It's an activity that brings you joy. It's something special that makes *you* happy," Émilie acknowledged as she scribbled notes.

"Exactly, and the same principle applies to your body and soul," Michelle continued. "As you know, I adore my garden. It brings me peace. The connection with the earth and God is rejuvenating. I also delight in helping our village elders. Remember how I go to the village to help Madame Vaillancourt?" her mother asked.

"Yes. You always go twice a week, on Wednesday and Sunday," answered Émilie.

"Well, since her husband died few months ago, she has not been the same. The time I spend with her chatting or helping with chores brings her joy. But talking to her and inspiring her brings happiness to me, as well," Michelle revealed.

Émilie understood the last principle. It was all about giving love back to yourself. It was about granting yourself the gift of self-appreciation.

⊰*French Secret*⊱

Life is journey, not a destination. Celebrate your accomplishments, big or small, in the spirit of self-appreciation.

"Thank you, *Maman*. You have given me lots of ideas on how to appreciate my mind and soul. What about my body? What would be a way to show appreciation to my body?" asked Émilie, looking for more advice.

"It's actually very simple. You need to think of what your body wants to receive from you as a gesture of love. For me, I keep myself fit and toned. My daily exercises keep me vigorous. I also like spending time making my body attractive for *Papa* and me. A woman's body is a beautiful gift from God, and we must take care of it. My daily bliss is also amazing for my body, mind, and soul. As you know, Émilie, *Papa* and I are very close and enjoy giving each other pleasure daily. It brings us closer emotionally and, well… we also have a lot of fun. It keeps our spirits in balance," Michelle disclosed with a gleam in her eye.

Émilie laughed, "Yes, it's true. *Papa* and you are like kids when you're together. You can't keep your hands off each other."

Michelle began to laugh along.

Émilie continued, "It's amazing to see you both so much in love with each other after all these years."

Michelle looked at her daughter earnestly. "This is why you must love yourself first and always. You cannot give what you do not possess. Self-love is the foundation of everything in life. It's the primary source of love and happiness. You can only love your soul mate if you love yourself. The only thing that is left to do is find someone that practices these same principles. You may not find the perfect match, but if the person is willing to learn, you can lead your relationship by example. The trick is to never settle for less than what you give. Not ever!

Émilie's head was spinning. It was like discovering a treasure at the bottom of the ocean. Suddenly life was full of possibilities. She was dedicated to finding her self-appreciation over the next couple of days. She had a few ideas from the conversation with her mother. She enjoyed reading and learning everything that caught her interest. She also enjoyed helping her family with the garden and farm. Émilie was thinking that perhaps it would be a great idea to go with her mother and see Madame Vaillancourt every Sunday, as well. As far as giving appreciation to her body, Émilie delighted in giving herself bliss every night before bed. She savored the moment and the moments afterward. It always brought her the best of dreams, looking at the angels with a smile. Émilie also had a favorite place near the lake where she would lie down naked and let the warm sun of southern France kiss her body as she caressed her femininity. She always found it magical the way the universe surrounded her.

⚘*French Secret*⚘

Being in love with who you are is fundamental for self-love in the French art de l'amour.

It had been some time since mother and daughter had had their last one-on-one conversation about the principles of self-love. Instead of talking about it, Émilie showed her learning through actions. Michelle was happy and most impressed with Émilie's progress in the French *art de l'amour*. Émilie's days were filled with happiness and love for everyone, including, most importantly, for herself. She did not complain about exterior events that influenced her life anymore. She no longer spoke about or dwelled upon past relationships. She now understood that she was completely responsible for her own actions and their outcomes. This new way of seeing life gave her an internal strength that she used throughout the day.

One day, Michelle found Émilie in the garden.

"*Comment vas-tu, mon ange?*" ("How are you, my angel?") Michelle asked.

"*Très bien, Maman. Mais je dois être très franche et avouer que je pense peut-être à partir pour quelque temps.*" ("Very good, Mother. But I must confess that I am thinking of leaving for a little while").

Michelle had known that this time would come soon. Émilie was twenty-one and she wanted to expand her self-discovery.

Émilie had been very happy since she discovered self-love. She had unearthed a great many things about herself. However, something was missing.

The Four Secret Rings of Love and Happiness

She wanted to find true love. She yearned to find a love that was beautiful and worthy of her new journey.

"Émilie," Michelle inquired, "*que veux-tu faire et ou veux-tu aller?*" ("What do you plan to do and where do you want to go?")

Émilie replied excitedly, "I would like to go to Paris for a while. I know the Germans occupy part of the city, but something tells me to go there."

Michelle was not thrilled with this sudden eagerness for adventure from her only child. However, she knew that she could not hold her back forever. She smiled at Émilie. She looked into her daughter's big blue eyes and took the silver ring off her own finger. Michelle had worn that ring for as long as she remembered.

"Here, Émilie," her mother said simply. She took Émilie's ring finger and slid the beautiful silver ring on it.

A tear ran down Émilie's cheek as Michelle added, "*Je suis très fière de toi, Émilie.*" ("I am very proud of you, Émilie. You are ready"). Émilie was shocked.

"When do you want to leave for Paris?" Michelle asked.

"Two weeks from today!"

Michelle looked at her daughter proudly. "Very well. Let's have a beautiful supper tonight with *Papa* to celebrate."

ᨄÉmilie's Journalᨄ

Dear Journal,

My first secret has been revealed to me! I am so excited and overjoyed that Maman gave me her beautiful silver ring. This special ring reminds me that I MUST start the day with self-love. This principle is so fundamental to love and happiness. By focusing on self-love every day, I feel happier, calmer, and centered in my soul. I feel purpose in my growth. I realize that true love of yourself is the key that opens all the doors to a loving relationship with yourself and others.

I have learned that in order to attract love the way I want to be loved, everything must start with ME. Being self-response-able for everything that happens to me gives me the power to change my life so I can live the way that I want. I have no reason to feel like a victim anymore. I am fully in charge of my own destiny.

When I put my silver ring on, I remind myself of five blessings that have been given to me. These self-affirmations make me feel blessed and also attract more of the same. I've found that the more I focus on what I want, the more I receive what I want.
One of my favorite principles is self-improvement. Right now, I am focusing on developing the best version of myself and BEING my own best friend. I keep myself honest to my true feelings. I also keep my word. Being trustworthy and dependable brings

me faith in my abilities. I'm also learning to listen and not judge. Too often, I've been quick to respond without taking the time to fully understand the message. Being empathetic is a beautiful gift. I also try not to take myself too seriously. I try to find humor and a lighter side to everything around me.

I've also discovered that I must self-forgive my imperfections. Nobody can claim to be perfect, including me. The ability to let go of the captive feelings of remorse, sadness, shame, and inferiority is liberating! By assuming full responsibility for everything that happens in my life, I've become empowered. It allows me to grow. I try to learn something positive from every failure and celebrate every victory. In fact, I am becoming thankful for failures because they provide me areas that I can learn from and grow upon.

The last principle of self-love is extremely grounding for me. Self-appreciation is easy. Every day, I think of one thing that gives my body, mind, and soul joy. I nourish my soul with daily acts of kindness, either by helping Maman *with dinner or* Papa *with the business. I take time to help others. These little acts of kindness fulfill my spirit. For my mind, I take some time to do activities that I really enjoy. I take time for myself so I can focus completely on me. Finally, I love taking care of my appearance since it has a huge impact on how I feel inside.* Maman *always tells me that my body is the temple of my soul. I also love giving my body joy every day. Bringing myself to bliss daily is amazing.*

I learn about what I like and dislike and enjoy these magnificent feelings. Every day, I explore a little bit more of my beautiful feminine sexuality.

☙

The Four Secret Rings of Love and Happiness

The Second Secret Ring

Intimacy *or* The Communion of the Souls

The French art of love-making is a sacred affair for French people. The stereotype comes from centuries of culture and refined education. The French see making love as experiencing the most succulent meal with your best friend. Everything is done with an attention to detail. The mood is purposefully set to enjoy this beautiful experience. Attention to detail and a slow pace are paramount. Savoring every moment is in order. There is no need to rush an incredible meal with amazing company, wouldn't you agree?

Communication, including the exchange of inner thoughts and desires, is crucial. Enjoying each other's beautiful gifts is the sole purpose.

The second secret, intimacy, can be broken down into three phases. The first one is courting or exercising chivalry (emotional). The second phase refers to romance or capturing each other's inner soul (spiritual), and finally, intimacy (physical), where the culmination of all three meld together, creating the ultimate experience: the communion of body and soul.

ಖ

The morning was like no other in the beautiful village of St. Girons. Nature was waking, and the birds and wild animals serenaded the birth of a new day. The sun was about to peak over the mountains, and fresh air filled the valley. The southern French village looked like a painting. It was an oasis of peace.

Émilie woke up spirited and full of hope. No sadness was in her heart or soul. She put on her silver ring and took some time to reflect on five blessings for which she was grateful. Following her daily affirmation, she thought of her self-improvement for the day. Since Émilie did not know what would happen beyond St. Girons, she decided that she would stay open to all of the blessings that would be granted that day.

Michelle and Émilie had been talking at length about her journey to Paris. The first *arrêt* (stop) would be Michelle's sister's house. It had been many years since she had seen her Aunt Cécile and Uncle Renée. She was only fourteen the last time she saw them. They were visiting Michelle en route to their vacation in Cote d'Azur.

Seven years had passed, and Cécile did not know how Émilie had matured. The young child she once knew, now a woman in control of her destiny, was about to discover the second secret ring of love and happiness.

Michelle, Ernest, and Émilie arrived at *la gare* (train station) at 6:10 a.m. She was surrounded by her loving family. Ernest suddenly broke into tears.

Seeing his beautiful daughter leaving for Paris in these troubled times filled his heart with sorrow.

"Ne pleure pas, Papa," ("Don't cry, Daddy,") uttered Émilie, taking her father's hand. "I will write you and *Maman* every day to let you know that I am safe and happy. I will tell you all about my new adventure."

Ernest still had difficulty containing himself. Michelle hugged him and gave him a warm kiss. "Be proud, my husband. You've done extraordinarily well with Émilie. It's her time now. She is ready to fly like a little bird leaving the nest."

Michelle knew how Émilie had grown. Self-love was now a part of her daily routine, and her life and her silver ring were there to prove it.

The 6:30 train en route to Limoges, (Limousin, southwest France) slowly approached. They could see the long plume of smoke rising above the treetops. The whistle reminded Michelle to bring the family to prayer.

"Let's pray," she said.

Émilie and Ernest bowed their heads.

"Dear Lord, please take this child under your care. Make her able to receive the abundance of your grace and have the courage to live as the strong woman she has become. Amen."

Steaming from all sides, the train came to rest at the station. The smell of burnt grease and coal filled the air. The heat was almost overwhelming. Suddenly, the conductor's whistle blew three times. A pressing voice urged the passengers to join him on board. Her new adventure was about to begin.

Émilie kissed her *papa* and *maman*. Tears of joy, excitement, and sadness rolled over her rosy cheeks. She carried only two suitcases with her. No need for more baggage when you have a positive mindset, Émilie thought. This new attitude was powerful. Her newfound knowledge of the five principles of self-love gave her the strength to enter the world.

Michelle stood by Émilie's side holding a brown package.

"*Voici*, Émilie. Here is a gift."

She reached out and took the gift. "*Merci beaucoup, Maman.*"

"It is a little gift for you, my love."

"*Qu'est-ce que c'est?*" Émilie asked.

"It's a magnificent journal and small gift from your father."

"Thank you, *Maman et Papa*! You are so kind!"
Ticket in hand, Émilie boarded the train and found her cabin. It was nicely decorated with red drapes

and brown leather seats. This will be perfect stage for my personal reflection, she thought.

Sitting comfortably, she heard the whistle and felt the rumble of the engine. Michelle and Ernest were outside her window, waving and wishing her good luck. She returned the gesture with excitement. Her new adventure was taking form. It was all up to her now. However, nothing had prepared her for what was about to come. This new journal was going to be very different. It had to be.

Émilie was very different now. She always wore a beautiful smile. Her mere presence could light up a room. Her focus and happiness was noticeable to everyone, even strangers. It seemed as if the world was smiling back at her as well. Her new journal would document the proof of that.

Soon the station was far away.

Only two hours before I see Aunty, Émilie thought.

She was happy and excited. Despite not seeing her in a long time, Cécile was, by far, her favorite aunt. She was her mother's oldest sister and, even though they had been separated by time and distance, Émilie felt very close to her.

"This new journal will be a testament to my new life," said Émilie with confidence as she unwrapped the beautiful gift.

Pulling the fine white strings that kept the brown wrapping paper together, she revealed a gorgeous bright red leather-bound journal with gold-leafed pages and her father's special fountain pen. Émilie smiled.

ɞFrench Secretɞ

It is not unusual to see a French person with their personal journal near the river Seine on a beautiful Sunday afternoon. Journaling is one of their favorite passe-temps *(pastimes). Besides being entertaining, the therapeutic benefit of documenting your thoughts, emotions, and moments of discovery is invaluable. The act of personal introspection is by far the greatest tool to personal growth.*

A few happy tears rolled down Émilie's cheek. She took her pink monogrammed handkerchief and wiped them gently away.

"No tears, anymore. I need to write," Émilie affirmed to herself.

As she opened the cover of her new journal, she noticed a note addressed to her.

Dear Love,

This is my gift to you. It served me well throughout the years and taught me so much. I am passing it on to you. It is now time to make it your own.

PS: I love you, xo

Maman

A huge smile grew on Émilie's face. It was not just like her mother's journal: it was her mother's journal, the very same! Émilie started to read some of the entries and recognized the self-love principles they spoke of.

"I will continue her journey," Émilie whispered softly.

She closed the journal, turned it over, and began to write from the last page forward.

"I will make her proud, and show her and *Papa* how God is leading me on my quest."

Dear Journal,

Today is the first day of my new life. Maman *has prepared me well for this adventure. Self-love has been a real breakthrough. The shadows and dark clouds that were once over me are now gone. As I assume complete responsibility for what is happening to me, I remind myself every day of the beautiful gift that I bring to the world.*

Émilie touched the silver ring that her mother gave her. She continued to write.

Today I choose to forgive and release anyone who didn't believe in me, including myself. I assume full responsibility and therefore release all my bad emotions back in to the universe.

As Émilie completed the sentence, she closed her eyes and imagined releasing a small bird from her hands.

"Fly. Fly away. I release you from my captive soul," she uttered, almost as if in prayer.

By this time the train was nearing Limoges. Her excitement grew. Soon she would see her aunty. Émilie tried to imagine how Cécile looked now.

Will she be able to recognize me? I hope she recognizes my red bow, she thought.

Michelle had written her sister two weeks before and mentioned that Émilie would be wearing a bright red ribbon in her hair when she arrived.

A knock on the door startled her from her thoughts.

"Good day, young lady, we will be at your destination in less than thirty minutes, the conductor said.
"*Merci, monsieur*," Émilie replied with a polite smile.

Émilie sighed as she put her journal and her *plume fontaine* (fountain pen) back in her leather bag, and thought of her *Papa* Ernest. He used his favorite pen whenever he came upon a crossword puzzle. Every Saturday morning, Ernest and Émilie had a ritual: they would walk together to the bistro a few blocks from where *Papa* always bought a *petit appéro*, and a *café au lait* for Émilie. They would sit together and exchange ideas, and then he would get his newspaper to tackle the special weekend crossword. He would sit and solve the puzzles by discovering the cryptic words, one-by-one, while Émilie played cards with a neighboring patron. Whenever he completed a crossword, he would raise his pen and declare victoriously, "This is magic! I've done it again!"

Limoges finally came into sight. Émilie could not contain her excitement. She picked up the leather bag that Ernest had made for her. From the window, she could see brown cows near the train station. A military regiment was rounding them up, keeping them away from the incoming train. Émilie could not tell if they were German or French soldiers. As the train slowly approached the station, she recognized the standard gray uniform and funny *casque d'acier* (steel helmet) of the French Army. A sigh of relief unwittingly escaped her. She noticed a heavily armed train approaching from the other direction, bearing the French flag at the front of the engine. Intrigued, she continued to watch. It must be the French Army or Resistance, she thought. The huge train, painted in camouflage, stopped in a most peculiar way: silently. It blew no whistle, had no lights, and spewed no steam. It seemed as if it was hiding from the enemy.

Émilie watched as a garrison of French Army soldiers got off the transport train. Pressed by their superior officer to exit, they quietly rushed out, grabbing rifles and backpacks along the way. All of them seemed nervous, yet focused. Suddenly she noticed a certain officer fast approaching her cabin. He was tall, with dark hair combed lavishly to the side. She became both excited and apprehensive at the same time. He was by far the most handsome young man that she had ever seen.

The French officer grabbed the door handle and stepped in. Émilie stepped back to allow him to enter.

"Bonjour, mademoiselle. Je suis le Lieutenant Antoine St. Germain de la Résistance Française Sud-Ouest." ("Good day, my lady. My name is Antoine St. Germain, lieutenant of the Southwest Resistance.")

Émilie could not answer. She tried to say her name but no words came out.

"I am sorry. It seems that I've frightened you," Antoine apologized.

Émilie was not afraid. She was under his spell. The young officer was magnificent. She had never seen so much confidence personified in a man before.

"No, sir, I am not afraid," Émilie replied, regaining her composure. "My name is Émilie Durant. I am from St. Girons. What is your regiment doing in Limoge?"

"We just arrived from fighting the Germans. We won the battle but many of my men have been wounded," Antoine replied sadly. "What are you doing in Limoges, *mademoiselle*?"

"I am here to visit my aunt Cécile on my way to Paris," Émilie explained.

"Very well, is there anything I can do to help you find your aunt?" Antoine offered.

"To be honest, I am a bit early. Perhaps I could surprise her by going to her house on my own," Émilie suggested.

"Consider it my order," said Antoine, coming to attention. "I will fetch my staff car."

Émilie could not contain her emotions. She felt so fearless and decisive. Yet, at the same time, she was quivering on the inside. Antoine ordered his regimental sergeant to fetch his car. A few minutes later, a black Citroen approached the cabin where Émilie and Antoine waited.

৶*French Secret*৶

The French know the importance of values and character when winning their love's heart. One must provide safety and a sense of emotional protection from a physical, emotional, and spiritual place. The chevalier *must also establish trust in his love's character. She must feel safe in order to open up to him.*

"Mademoiselle, your chariot has arrived," Antoine announced with a half-bow. He jumped off the train, turned around, and extended his arms to assist Émilie. He wanted to make sure she was not hurt while stepping down.

"Thank you so much, Lieutenant St. Germain," Émilie said politely.

"Please, call me 'Antoine'. I am here to serve you," he responded valiantly.

Émilie had never felt so safe. His kindness and sensitivity melted her fear and filled her heart.

"Antoine, can we go now? I really want to surprise my aunt," Émilie requested politely.

"*Bien sur*, Émilie. *Voici, mademoiselle*," he replied, opening the rear passenger door and helping her into the car. One of Antoine's corporals drove. His accent was from the *midi* of France. It was obvious that Antoine and his driver were good friends and brothers in arms.

"Émilie, where does your aunt live?" Antoine asked.

Émilie retrieved her journal from her leather bag, "Just a moment, I have a note from *Maman*," Émilie answered as she leafed through the pages.

"You have a beautiful journal, Émilie. I have one, too, you know. Every day, I record what is happening on the battlefield so the younger generation can appreciate what *Les Maquis* have done for France," he said proudly. Émilie smiled. She was extremely impressed by this man. "Here, Antoine, I have the address. It is 49 *avenue de la Rose*," Émilie read.

"Very well. You heard Mademoiselle, Robert?" he asked his driver.

"*Oui, bien sur*," Robert replied with a nod.

ꙮFrench Secretꙮ

Nothing turns your potential love off more quickly than a weak and indecisive character. People require emotional and physical stability, as well as protection. Man up (even if you're a woman)!

Happiness and laughter filled the little Citroen. The war seemed very distant at the moment. Antoine and Robert were gallant with Émilie. Both made sure she felt at ease and protected. Then, turning the corner onto *avenue de la Rose*, Émilie noticed the door sign: 49. It was a charming house with a beautiful red door. It was obvious that Aunt Cécile had a knack for gardening like her *maman*. The front of the house was covered with a variety of roses: red, pink, white and yellow.

"*Voici*, we are here," Robert announced. Émilie could not contain her emotions. She rushed out of the car, jumping with joy and with the wind in her steps. Antoine could barely keep up with her. Her spirit and energy were contagious. Émilie pranced to the red door and knocked three times. She heard her aunt inside talking to Renée. Then Émilie knocked upon the door again.

Émilie shouted, "*Ma Tante* Cécile, it is me, please open the door." Then she heard Cécile scream with joy at the sound of her voice.

Cécile ran from the kitchen and swung the front door open. Without saying a word, they kissed each other on both cheeks, laughed, and wept with joy. When they finally returned to their senses, they had been hugging for what seemed like five minutes.

"Émilie, you are so tall and beautiful!" said Cécile with pure emotion in her voice.

"My dear aunt, you look so young. I love your hairstyle," Émilie replied, returning the compliment. The style Cécile wore was the classic look of famous movie actresses of the late 1930's.

"Did you have a good trip?" asked Cécile.

"Yes, it was lovely. I had a chance to write in my journal that *Maman* gave me before I left," Émilie recounted.

Cécile smiled. "A journal? We will have to talk about this. I can't wait to hear all about it, if you are ok with sharing your thoughts," Cécile suggested in an inquisitive yet comforting voice.

"Aunty, I would like to present to you Lieutenant St. Germain de la Résistance Française and his corporal, Robert. They brought me here in their staff car. Their kindness and chivalry have been exemplary," Émilie said proudly.

Antoine stepped up to the porch with Robert. He took Cécile's hand and kissed it. "*Enchanté*, Madame. I am Lieutenant St. Germain and this is my aid, Corporal Vaillancourt. Please call me 'Antoine'," the Lieutenant announced.

"Welcome to our home," Cécile greeted them both. "Thank you so much for bringing Émilie to us. She was only fourteen last time we saw her. It's amazing what seven years can do. She is so tall and beautiful now," Cécile boasted.

"Yes, very true," Antoine agreed.

"What is your regiment doing in Limoges?" Cécile asked, intrigued.

"We have just returned from battle with the Germans. We are the *Maquis du Limousin*," Antoine explained in an official tone.

"What a great honor to have you here. I've read your stories of valor in the newspaper in detail," Cécile admitted.

"I wouldn't believe everything that the newspaper says about us," Antoine replied with a humble smile.

"Is it true that you pushed out two platoons of Wehrmacht from Saint-Jouvent with only fifteen men?" Cécile asked.

"Yes, it is true but we were twenty, plus myself, to be precise. Five of my men were wounded. No casualties, thankfully," said Antoine with a distant sadness in his voice.

"If Émilie agrees, I would like to invite you for dinner tonight. You are, after all, a French hero. Please invite your troops and we will roast one of our pigs in celebration of your bravery," Cécile requested excitedly.

"Very well. We would be honored to celebrate with you, with Émilie's permission, of course. It can be a double celebration. Today is my aid Robert's birthday. He is twenty-two and still can't grow a moustache," Antoine chuckled.

Robert laughed as well, brushing at his few facial hairs.

Antoine and Robert walked down the pathway to their staff car. It was now 10:00. The troops, Robert and Antoine were due to be back at 18:00.

Émilie and Cécile laughed and renewed their bonds.

"So tell me, Émilie, how is your *maman*? I haven't heard from her since the letter she sent last month, announcing your arrival," Cécile said.

"She's doing very well. You know *Maman*, always upbeat and happy. She still spends most of her time tending to the garden and, of course, she still practices self-love every day," Émilie answered with admiration.

"Yes, Michelle and I were taught the importance of self-love by our mother," Cécile reflected.

Émilie was surprised. She thought that only her mother, Michelle, knew about the five principles.

"You know, Émilie, self-responsibility and self-affirmation is my kimberlite stone," Cécile said with a tone of accomplishment.

"Your kimberlite stone? What do you mean,

Aunty?" Émilie asked, furrowing her brow.

"A kimberlite stone represents a difficult point of your journey. Breaking through, it brings you a beautiful diamond," Cécile explained. "Typically, the aspect you have the most difficulty resolving and implementing into your daily life becomes a cornerstone of your development," she continued.

Émilie was pensive. "I guess my kimberlite stone was self-responsibility" Émilie admitted, somewhat ashamed.

"It's amazing that you recognize this at your age. It took me quite a while before I discovered what mine was," Cécile confessed. "How do you feel now that you have broken through this hard stone?"

"It feels like I've discovered a diamond to cherish," Émilie beamed. "Knowing that the outcome of my life is entirely my responsibility gives me power and strength over my own judgment and character. Feeling in control of my own future helps me appreciate who I am and who I am becoming. In the beginning, it was difficult to say and affirm five things to be thankful for every day. Now I catch myself smiling, putting on my ring, and reminding myself what I am grateful for," Émilie proudly stated. "It gives me wings that lift me for the day."

Cécile was impressed by her niece. She was only twenty-one and well on her way to mastering all of the self-love principles.

While Cécile and Émilie caught up, Renée prepared the pork for the evening's feast. Cécile had a few acres of some of the best wine grapes in the region, so great wine was also on the menu for the evening. Cabernet Sauvignon was their specialty. They had won the 1937 regional Limoges French Wine of the Year. Their "Cab" was to be enjoyed that evening. They also had a few cows from which they got fresh milk each morning. They made the most succulent cheese and butter, which was a secret recipe passed down from Michelle and Cécile's mom.

It was now 17:11, and the troops were getting ready to have a wonderful time and great food. Everyone was brushing their uniform and securing the camp before their departure. Antoine was thinking about Émilie and how incredible he thought she was. He was hoping to be worthy of her love. He knew that courting her was about being *chevaleresque* and showing, with action, his worth to her by providing grounds for her trust. His word would be his badge of honor. Providing protection from physical, emotional, and spiritual harm was crucial.

Finally, the troops boarded their grey transport truck en route to Cécile and Renée's farm. The atmosphere was festive. Laughter and song filled the back of the truck. Having been in the field and facing death for so many months left them all thirsty for safety and comfort. It was a well needed break, and a relief for all of them. They yearned for a time when war did not exist and human candor prevailed.

"We're almost there," called out the truck driver in a loud and enthusiastic voice. The troops continued to sing and paid no attention. Antoine and Robert led the convoy. They had brought some food with them to share but, more importantly, they had also brought their gift of music and *joie de vivre*. A few had been professional singers and musicians before the war. They had brought their instruments with them and were excited to have a normal, peaceful night again.

The last time had been seven months earlier when they arrived in Limoges. The mayor had organized a welcoming party for the "Defenders of France". At the time, none of them had seen action in the field. Now these boys were men. They were battle-hardened brothers in arms and knew each other very well.

"*Nous sommes arrivé!*" said the driver to the troops. The truck stopped in front of Cécile's house. It was 18:00 sharp—military precision. The Lieutenant was already at the house when the troops arrived. Antoine and Émilie, side by side, were standing with Cécile, Renée, Robert, and the neighbors to greet their heroes.

One by one, the soldiers jumped off the back of the truck, bringing their instruments with them. They each kissed their welcoming party on both cheeks (except for Lieutenant St. Germain, of course: they simply smiled and saluted him).

"Come on, my friends! Follow me, and we will celebrate!" Cécile called out excitedly. The troops, led by Lieutenant St. Germain, followed Cécile to the back of the farmhouse.

"I am so happy, Antoine," Émilie said excitedly.

"Me, too," Antoine agreed, brushing his hand against Émilie's. Without saying a word, Émilie's hand opened to receive Antoine's. Their romance had begun. Émilie felt very safe with Antoine. His genuinely caring and *chevaleresque* nature had melted her heart. She trusted him. He made her feel secure with herself by accepting her the way she was, without pretention. She felt that Antoine was potentially worthy of her love.

Émilie's soul and her gallant officer were starting to bond. They felt close to each other. It was still too early to say if romance was about to develop naturally. However, Antoine's courting was perfect for Émilie: gentle and reassuring. Émilie had never been in love before. She had had a few contenders, but she had never loved or knew what it felt like to be loved by a real man. She also did not know how to respond to love or romance, for that matter. Guidance would be required by her French officer. Self-love would be her foundation for a nurturing, healthy and loving relationship.

✄French Secret✄

Romance is about making time for love and for each other. If you were to walk along la Seine *in Paris at around 9:00 p.m. you would understand right away. Paris is a romantic city. The* splendeur *and* joie de vivre *of Paris, and France in general, is about romance and living love (spiritually).*

Cécile and Renée's farm was beautiful. It was Renée's father's legacy. It was well maintained and profitable. Many people considered it to be the reference point of the small village. Cows, pigs, goats, sheep, horses, and chickens made the *ménagerie* of its landscape. Everyone knew how to live harmoniously with each other.

The troops walked, one by one, to the backyard, singing regimental songs. Some soldiers carried their guitars, some carried trumpets. The evening was destined to be memorable for everyone. The roast was almost ready, and the smell of good food and a feeling of jubilation filled the air.

As everyone acquainted themselves with their new-found paradise, Émilie went to every guest and offered them wine and cheese. Soon the music started to intertwine with the laughter. It was a beautiful air of *Guitant* (Roma) jazz. There were four guitars and two trumpets feeding the merriment. Antoine helped Renée and another neighbor turn the spit while Émilie and Cécile prepared the table. Everyone was enjoying themselves. Antoine liked seeing Émilie laughing and happy. He was developing deep feelings for her. It seemed as if she was the only woman in the world.

Suddenly, Renée shouted through the music, "*Allez, mes amies*, our roast is ready!"

Everyone applauded. By this time, their guests were hungry. Wine had flowed and now it was time to appreciate their host's grace. Renée and Antoine were in charge of carving the portions right off the spit. One by one, each guest came around to get their share of the perfectly cooked, golden roast. When they gathered around the table they found vegetables, freshly made cheese, bread, butter, and more wine. As everyone prepared to sit, Antoine stood up and called for attention. As the laughter and rumbling wound down, Antoine cleared his throat and began to say grace.

"Dear friends and brothers in arms, today we would like to give thanks and show our appreciation to our hosts, Cécile, Renée, and Émilie. We thank them for their generosity and kindness. Your *Défenseur de la Republic* say 'thank you'. None of us have seen our families for many months now. Tonight, thanks to you, we remember that family is everything. On that note, I invite you all to raise your glasses and celebrate our Motherland. *Vive la France, Vive la France Libre!*"

All at once, everyone stood and yelled, "*Vive la France Libre!*"

Cécile briskly stood up beside the Lieutenant and responded to his toast with a patriotic flair. "*Merci*, Lieutenant St. Germain, for your wonderful speech. I agree with you that family is the most important thing and, with this in mind, I would like to invite your troops to stay here at the farm until your next deployment, with your permission."

Everyone was delighted by Cécile's proposition. Émilie could barely contain her joy.

Antoine added to Cécile's declaration. "Thank you, Cécile, for this generous offer. Before I can say yes, I will need to get confirmation from our headquarters. However, *Captaine* Dubois is a good friend of mine, and I cannot see why he would refuse this request."

The guests were thrilled. Antoine looked at Émilie with a smile. She blushed shyly back at him in anticipation.

Everyone was eating, singing, and laughing. Music filled the air. As it began to get dark, the guests surrounded the fire pit. Antoine and Émilie wandered away from the festivities to walk off their feast.

"A little exercise should do us good," Antoine said to Émilie.

She was comfortable with him. She felt safe and protected physically, emotionally, and spiritually. Émilie brushed the Lieutenant's hand this time. Antoine responded by holding her hand firmly but softly.

The farm had a path that led around the various buildings on the property. They walked slowly and gazed at the stars. It was a magical southwest France summer sky. It seemed as if millions of candles lit the darkness just for them. Antoine and Émilie spoke about their pasts, strengthening their bond. They also talked about what they wanted to do after the war was over. Antoine did not have big dreams to share.

"In war, you never know if today is the last. It makes you better appreciate the present moment," said Antoine with wisdom.

Émilie understood.

Then the Lieutenant stopped Émilie and kissed her gently under the stars. It was their first kiss, a preparatory kiss. Émilie did not refuse him. She could barely stand after that. Silence surrounded them as if in honor of the romance that was developing. Their courtship had all the elements of a strong and passionate union.

Then Antoine asked Émilie a question that surprised her in many ways. "What is your secret to happiness?

You always seem to be happy and smiling."

"Self-love," she replied.

Antoine had not expected that answer but, at the same time, had an idea of what Émilie was referring too. "I like that answer. When you say 'self-love', what exactly do you mean?" he asked, genuinely interested.

"Self-love was taught to me by my *maman*. She always used the example of her garden to explain the different aspects of self-love," Émilie explained with a touch of nostalgia in her voice.

"My mother also loves gardening. Roses are her favorite," Antoine noted, surprisingly emotional with his answer.

"I bet they could be good friends," Émilie smiled.

"Tell me more," Antoine requested.

"*Maman* always accepts responsibility for the outcome of her life. Also, every morning as she puts on her special silver ring, she reminds herself of five blessings that she is grateful for or happy about. Then she reflects on her accomplishments. She calls it 'self-affirmation'."

"Do you do that too, Émilie?" Antoine asked.

"Yes. Like her, when I put on my silver ring, I

remind myself of five things that I am grateful for. I also try to always accept responsibility for what is happening to me. This way I never feel like a victim and am always empowered with my choices," Émilie explained.

"Is this your mother's ring?" Antoine asked, holding her hand.

"Yes. She gave it to me after my last breakthrough," Émilie said proudly. "It's getting late now, Antoine, we should go back. I can continue to explain my secret next time," Émilie invited coyly.

"You're right, Émilie. Did you enjoy our...?" Antoine paused.

"Yes, I really like your kiss Antoine. I had butterflies in my stomach," Émilie blushed.

"I really like your smile, Émilie. You are very beautiful."

"Thank you, Antoine. You are *chevaleresque*. You make me feel at ease and safe," Émilie said shyly. She had never opened up like this to a man before. The feeling was strange and euphoric.

"I am your knight to serve you, my lady," Antoine laughed, giving a little bow.

Then he took Émilie's hand and led her back to the farm.

It was now well into the night and the troops had to leave. The next morning would be occupied by preparations for their move. They were quiet during transit back to their camp. Limoges had a few reported German spies in the village. Antoine sat with his troops in the back of the truck to make sure that everyone was absolutely silent for the trip back. The troops quietly thought of the magic moments they had just shared. They looked at each other without making direct eye contact.

Antoine's heart was racing. Being close to Émilie felt like a gift from God. Just the thought of it filled his heart with possibilities. They were the kind of dreams that one can only have after a war. Future plans with her would have to be on hold. However, his heart was saying something very different. Their romance and the feeling in their souls was real, but the heart does not understand how human tragedy and world conflict could deny its desires.

Finally, they arrived at the camp without incident. The injured soldiers and medical personnel who stayed behind received a huge surprise. Antoine and the rest of the platoon had brought them food and drink. Satisfied and happy, they rested for the night while Antoine organized the night patrol. His men looked up to him. He had gained their trust and respect by always holding to his word.

Antoine used to say that his word was the only thing he really had and he would guard it with his life. His integrity was important to the men. Romance also needs these same personal values in order to take root. He had the values of a modern day knight, and Émilie recognized and embraced it.

Soon, morning rose over the camp. Nothing troubled the sleep of the troops. Nothing unusual, that is. One corporal on patrol reported some activities near the woods. It could have been some German scouts but none were discovered. There was also a cow. Some of the farmers near the camp allowed their animals to roam free at night. For the past few nights a cow, affectionately known as "Betsy", came to the camp to visit the sugar storage. Two soldiers took her back to the pasture that morning.

The sun was shining, and life around the camp was in full swing. Everyone was eagerly anticipating bugging out and becoming a part of the community surrounding Cécile's farm. They offered a sense of protection against the invading forces. Antoine received permission from headquarters to move to Cécile's farm for the next two weeks, before they were to be deployed near Paris.

They tore down their camp and packed it onto trucks. The field kitchen was to be put on last so the men could have their usual *potage* (soup) before departing for good. The soup was, basically, whatever they could find around the camp that was nutritious. Oftentimes, the local farmers offered something to stew. They were, after all, the *Défenseur de la Patrie*.

Renée, Cécile, and Émilie were active preparing the farm to receive the soldiers. They were not many in total, just twenty-one, including Antoine. However, they would need some support. Water, firewood, pots, and pans were gathered to help them. Accommodations would be on the premises. The four buildings, not including the house, would be used for shelter.

Émilie was daydreaming. She was constantly thinking about Antoine, her handsome French officer, though she still kept to her daily practice of self-love. She learned that she needed to love herself before she could extend that gift to any other person. During her self-affirmation practice, she gave thanks that Antoine was present for her. She was also grateful for her Aunt Cécile and Uncle Renée's generosity.

Émilie also set herself an objective as part of her self-improvement practice. She would learn something new about Antoine's life and character every day. She did not know, at the time, that she would discover the second secret ring, intimacy. Antoine would be her guide and mentor on this part of the French *art de l'amour* journey.

At 12:30 p.m. Cécile, Renée, and Émilie were still preparing the house and surroundings of the farm for the arrival of the troops. They heard rumbling noises, coming from afar, that seemed to be growing louder. The approaching convoy was only a few blocks away. Two trucks and one staff car approached. One of the trucks carried an artillery piece with a grey canvas tarp over it. The field kitchen was also in the back of this truck. In front of it, a transport truck carried the troops. The mood of the soldiers was of celebration and certain peace once again. They would finally live a somewhat normal life for the next two weeks.

Antoine and Robert led the convoy in the staff car. Antoine was particularly happy. His heart was growing with passion and desire for Émilie and their romantic journey.

When the troops arrived, the atmosphere was almost like a town carnival as they erected their camp at the back of the farm. Everyone knew their role, as hundreds of times before when they had set up camp. Antoine was the grand "maestro". Émilie helped him with the troops. The field kitchen was to be put near the fire pit. The artillery piece, still under the tarp, was hidden in one of the buildings to avoid unwanted attention.

Everyone was settled as the day came to an end. The cook prepared his famous *ratatouille*, a feast the troops always appreciated. Antoine planned his military maneuvers for the next morning. Every day, a certain amount of time was dedicated to training his soldiers. Tomorrow wouldn't be any different. His favorite was *embuscade* (patrol attack). Adopting his tactics to guerrilla-style warfare was crucial due to the limited number of men he had. He had some difficulty concentrating, though. All of the daily exercises seemed a bit futile. The Germans were retreating from France and the war would soon be over. Émilie occupied Antoine's heart and filled his thoughts. He was looking forward to spending quality time with her and growing the love between them.

"Will you walk with me under the stars tonight, Émilie?" Antoine requested hopefully.

"Of course, Antoine, after I finish the daily chores with my aunt," Émilie replied. "You know, my aunt and uncle really like you. They find you very gallant," Émilie admitted.

"And you, do you like me?" Antoine prodded.

"Yes, very much! Each day that I am with you, your *chevaleresque* character secures my heart and my feelings grow for you," Émilie blushed. This was the first time she really opened up to Antoine. In fact, it was the first time she ever let her heart speak to any man.

Antoine and Émilie were inseparable. She helped *la Résistance* with the camp basics while Antoine exercised his troops during the day. The troops also helped other farms around the village with much needed renovations and maintenance. It was a great time in Limoges. The troop band entertained the village nightly from 18:00 to often 21:00 at the *place du marché* (center of the town).

Émilie and Antoine explored each other and fell in

love more and more every day. Antoine was leading and teaching Émilie about the secret of intimacy.

ೞFrench Secretೞ

Sharing personal insight, thought, and future aspirations is the founding ground of "shared common goals and values". It is also a very important aspect of the romantic phase, compatibility.

Each night, Antoine and Émilie walked together. They talked about their pasts and strengthened their soul-tie, building their spiritual intimacy. They also talked about what they wanted to do after the war was over.

Then the Lieutenant put his hand around Émilie's waist, guiding her to him. Under the stars, they exchanged a simple kiss. A preparatory kiss. Émilie did not refuse him. Silence surrounded them and bathed them in their romantic bliss.

ೞFrench Secretೞ

Romance is a form of mature courting where two souls give each other the gift of time to discover and tighten up the bond of love from a physical, emotional, and spiritual perspective.

By the fourth evening of the arrival of the troops, the camp was running smoothly in its daily and evening routines. Later that night, Émilie and

Antoine, holding hands, went to a nearby pond. This secret place had become their favorite rendezvous. As they watched the sunset dive into the water, they became lost in each other's arms. It was a safe and private haven to grow their spiritual love.

Antoine had brought a beautiful blanket with him. It was a gift from his mother before he departed for the front line. Skillfully crafted from cashmere and wool, the soft red and white blanket became their landing place. It was their magic carpet. Antoine spread it on the ground as Émilie opened a bottle of wine and served cheese with fresh baguette.

Antoine always made sure that Émilie was comfortable and attended to her every need. He always offered the first glass of wine to her. Putting down the bottle, he slowly approached Émilie's lips. She welcomed him with an open heart. Still tasting the wine from her lips, they embraced passionately for what seemed like an eternity. Nothing else mattered. Antoine was the perfect embodiment of French romance. Their kisses felt like fireworks. This embrace would set the tone for the love that was to come.

Lying on the blanket, they admired the beautiful French sky together. Antoine's hands were gentle over Émilie's body. Feeling secure, cared for, and respected, she continued to open up to him.

ᛤ*French Secret*ᛤ

French approach the art of love-making like a beautiful meal to be enjoyed slowly. Love-making is an art, not a technique. The French favor the playfulness of the experience over the emptiness and shallow selfishness of the simple sexual act.

Antoine's fingers ran though her hair like a comb through silk. Not a word was said. Their eyes were locked in the motionless fabric of love. As he kissed her gently down her neck, Émilie let out a gasp of pleasure and surrendered to Antoine's lips. Slowly going down, he unbuttoned her dark blue and white flowered blouse. She was trembling with passion and anticipation. His mouth flowed over her erect nipple. His warm kiss was only subdued by the twirling of his tongue around her areola. Émilie was gasping for air. She had never felt euphoric pleasure like this before. Antoine was leading her gently to heaven. His finger was brushing gently over her other breast making her nipple rise in excitement. Tenderly, Émilie caressed Antoine's hair, encouraging him to go further.

He fulfilled her desire. Émilie's body was perfect.

ᛤ*French Secret*ᛤ

Self-love taught her that a positive self-image reinforces self-appreciation.

She had difficulty catching her breath, her

excitement was compounding. She allowed the beautiful experience to overcome her. Then, Antoine slowly ran the tips of his fingers over her smooth belly, discovering the edge of her magic garden. He felt her flowering Eden. Émilie was extremely aroused as she felt his tender touch on her quivering femininity.

ஐ*French Secret*ஐ

The French Art of Love-Making is selfless in its essence. One takes their greatest pleasure out of satisfying the other.

Antoine's fingers flowed over her drenched mound. Her blond pubic hair was soaked with joy. She grew closer and closer to exploding as Antoine led her to paradise.

"Let me taste," begged Émilie, half-conscious and intoxicated with pleasure. Antoine obeyed and gave her his fingers. She took them, one by one, and sucked them passionately. While Émilie enjoyed herself, Antoine gently kissed her secret garden. Émilie felt the warmth of Antoine's mouth and pushed her hips towards him, her body begging for more pleasure. Antoine was elated to satisfy her. He wanted nothing more than to pleasure her. Once more, his *chevaleresque* character shone through. He slowly took his moistened finger from Émilie's mouth and opened her beautiful rose petals. He gently teased her protruding clitoris and licked her slowly up and down in sync with her swaying body.

He listened as she called for more. 'Round and 'round, the tip of his tongue played with her before plunging inside to taste her sweet nectar. He was also on the verge of ecstasy but that was not important to him. Émilie's pleasure was all that mattered. His heartbeat thundered as her excitement grew. She drew closer and closer to overwhelming pleasure. Émilie was ready to bless him with an orgasm. As soon as Antoine introduced his middle finger inside her, she let out a moan of pleasure. Antoine pressed his tongue harder on her clitoris to accentuate the intensity. Émilie arched her back and let her love explode. Her entire body quaked. It was the first time she had reached that level of ecstasy. Antoine's passion gave her a taste of her natural purity and desire. He was teaching her the second secret of the French art of love-making, intimacy.

ಊ*French Secret*ಊ

The French art of love-making differs immensely from any other type of intimacy. The French have known this secret for many centuries. For them, making love and being intimate with their loved one is about "The Communion of the Soul". Every word of this statement is critical to understand, where the sum is greater than its parts. Please read this again. If your soul is not in communion with your loved one when you are intimate, you are not practicing the French art of love-making.

They lay together on Antoine's blanket, Émilie's head resting peacefully on his chest. She had immensely enjoyed the beautiful gift he had given her. Something within her changed at that moment. A new journey was upon her. She was growing from the inside out, like a chrysanthemum ready to bloom. She was becoming a woman, a woman ready to receive the second secret to love and happiness.

Émilie and Antoine had become soul tied, connected in all aspects of their intimacy. He had been at Cécile's farm for just over two weeks and was already considered a "member" of the viscount's family. Antoine and Émilie took time to cultivate a strong bond, a communion of soul, which only grows with openness and trust. Antoine was very knowledgeable in the French art of love-making. He was five years older than Émilie and passionate about all the discoveries that love
brought. He had had his heart broken more than once before but never felt resentment. He had felt used—more than once—for his fantastic qualities and character, but never felt pity for himself. Love and, more specifically, the art of love-making are selfless. Antoine was also an avid practitioner of self-love. Like Émilie, he had a daily self-love ritual that his mother had taught him.

One morning, Antoine received new orders from headquarters. He was to scout a forward observation post, outside Limoges. It was an important village to secure. Its geographic position was of great military importance. The town was at the crossroads of three important cities. It was the most likely route for the German army to retreat. The Resistance were to delay their fallback until the Allies captured them. The mission was crucial for the Resistance and for France. Antoine was torn. His new love for Émilie grew every day, and the thought of leaving her was almost impossible to bear.

"I must leave for two weeks to scout a location, Émilie," Antoine said flatly, trying to mask his emotions.

"Take me with you," implored Émilie.

"Impossible. You must stay with your family and my troops."

She continued assertively, ignoring what he said. "I want to be with you, Antoine. Everyone must do their part for the Motherland and I can be a second set of eyes for you," Émilie said with a smile.

The Lieutenant was conflicted; his love for her and his sense of protection could not allow her to be hurt for a war that she did not deserve. "Émilie, I would love to, but I must protect you. It is my duty and honor to do so," Antoine explained compassionately, his *chevaleresque* nature shining through once again.

That evening Émilie and Antoine went, holding hands, to their special place. They explored each other, Antoine leading her. Every day for the past week, he had taught her more and more about the

French art of love-making. She welcomed the incredible experience. Every day, she blessed him with an immense explosion of pleasure. Antoine's focus was on her alone.

ஐFrench Secretஐ

The French art of love-making is about keeping an open mind to the experience that is in front to you. When respect and dignity are present, nothing can do you harm.

The next day before dawn, Antoine left the farm in silence. No one knew where he was going, not even his sergeant. It was top secret information and he could not comprise the mission. He knew it was his duty during these times to put his feelings aside and dedicate himself to the greater cause. Driving under the cover of darkness without headlights, Antoine crept towards the scouting position like a cat in the night.

Suddenly, he heard a giggle from the back seat. He instantly recognized his angel's laugh. It was impossible. Émilie was back at the farm with her family. A burst of laughter came again from the back seat. He was not dreaming. He stopped the car at the side of the road. Stepping out of the car, he moved his seat forward to see what was making this noise, hoping for the best. As he looked back, he recognized the big blue eyes.

"No. Émilie. What are you doing? This is a very

dangerous mission," Antoine said in a stern whisper.

"I want to be with you," she replied. "I am an amazing scout, Antoine, and I will listen to your every command. I promise," she said, smiling.

"I can't turn back now to take you home. I need to be there shortly to make radio contact with headquarters." He was noticeably conflicted. "Please hide behind the seat until we're there. Try to get some sleep. The day will be tiring," Antoine suggested in a commanding manner.

Émilie went back under the blanket and rested for a while. Antoine got back on the road, once again, without headlights or noise. It would take another hour before they arrived at their destination.

The sun was starting to peek over the mountains and burn away the morning mist when they arrived at the scouting location. It was a regular farmhouse that had been abandoned. The location was perfect: near the crossroads yet hidden behind some other houses. It also had a great exit route, in case they needed to depart suddenly. Antoine got out of the staff car, making sure not to wake Émilie. He cautiously approached the house with his service pistol in hand and checked to see if the location was safe. The door was locked. He quickly broke a window near the door, slid his hand in, and unlocked it. Very aware that the Germans might have planted explosives, he entered with extreme caution. He secured the quaint dwelling one room at a time. The house looked great. All the amenities were intact and in good condition. Antoine was excited and apprehensive but most of all... in love. It was a love that would blossom into the most incredible passionflower. This house would become Antoine and Émilie's love nest.

Antoine went back to the staff car to find Émilie waking.

"Have we arrived, Antoine?" she asked softly.

"Yes, but we need to be careful. We have to keep our voices down and enter from the rear of the house," Antoine cautioned, leading her by the hand.

After they entered the house Émilie stood in the kitchen.

"Are you scared?" Antoine asked, noticing the trepidation in her.

Émilie took a breath and answered bravely, "Not when I am with you."

Antoine gently took her hands and pulled her against him. She was trembling with excitement. Antoine looked into her ocean blue eyes and blessed her with a passionate kiss. Then they made love on the kitchen table.

"Would you like to take a bath with me?" Antoine suggested.

Émilie simply nodded in agreement. She was speechless, excited, and welcomed the new experience. She had never taken a bath with a man before. Once again, Antoine led her in the French art of love-making.

ஐ*French Secret*ஐ

The French really take time for love and connecting with their loved one on a daily basis. A "love bath" is the perfect opportunity to relax, talk about the day, and cherish each other's body. Champagne on ice is also a nice complement!

"The bath is upstairs. Would you please draw the water while I hide the staff car in the barn?" Antoine asked.

"Yes, sir!" She saluted, pretending to be one of his troops.

Antoine gave her a quick kiss and then slid out the door.

Émilie watched him through the window for a moment, then went upstairs to draw the bath and discover the new house. The beautiful little house was surprisingly clean. Émilie wanted to respect their home. She took great care not to disturb the surroundings. Modestly decorated, it looked a bit like her parent's house. She felt at home and comfortable there with Antoine.

The bathroom was also nice. Everything had been left: towels, *savon de Provence* with a scent of lavender, and some red candles. It also had watery soap that she used to have luxury baths with at home. It was the type that mixed with water to make a scented foam. Fortunately, the owner had a water heater as well. This was very helpful for drawing a hot bath rather than having to boil it.

Émilie prepared the bathroom. She turned on the water to the perfect temperature and put in some of the watery soap. A beautiful scent slowly filled the room. Breathing it in deeply, she felt her excitement climb. She lit three candles and placed them near the bath. The room was perfect. She was also learning the French art of love-making by setting the right conditions for intimacy.

Émilie heard Antoine in the kitchen. There was a particular way that he walked. It sounded like he was searching for something.

"Antoine, I am here in the bathroom," Émilie called out, trying not to raise her voice.

"I will be there in a second, my love," replied Antoine in a loud whisper.

Émilie could hear Antoine going through the kitchen cupboards. He was trying to be quiet.

"Émilie, I have a surprise for you," he said excitedly. She heard some strange clanging as he climbed the stairs which piqued her curiosity.

ಽ*French Secret*ಽ

Oftentimes a change of location or adding romanticism to your daily life brings new emotions and a new perspective to love.

Guided by the light of the candles, Antoine entered the bathroom. Émilie could not believe what she saw.

"Champagne and a saber!" Émilie shrieked, grasping her mouth to hold back her laughter and the volume of her voice.

"I found the bottle in the *vaisselier* (wine cellar). It is a 1923 Grand Crue, and the Napoleonic saber was near the staircase close to the dish closet," Antoine said, giggling.

"What are you going to do with that saber, Antoine?" Émilie asked curiously.

"My darling, we have an old tradition that we used to practice in the officer's mess when I was in Paris. The French Hussars of Napoleon created this tradition. They used to cut off the head of the champagne bottle with their saber to celebrate victory.

If I recall, the *Champagnerie Veuve Cocliquot* was their favorite place to celebrate," he explained proudly.

"Are you going to try?" Émilie asked.

"Of course. This occasion is cause for celebration, would you not agree?" Antoine asked confidently.

Émilie was overwhelmed by Antoine's gallantry.

"Please take these champagne glasses while I saber this bottle," Antoine said, handing her the two champagne flutes.

Émilie could not believe what was about to happen. It was another first for her.

Antoine took the magnificent French saber in one hand and the champagne bottle in the other. "I would like to dedicate this wine to you. May this magical moment live forever," Antoine announced with bravado. Then, looking carefully at the weak point of this 1923 bottle, the officer ran his blade alongside it and cut off the head. Champagne triumphantly emerged as he quickly took Émilie's glass and poured the golden nectar.

ꙮ*French Secret*ꙮ

There is nothing more sensual, when practicing the French art of love-making, than sabering a bottle of champagne to celebrate love.

Émilie was under his magical spell of showmanship. She was falling for him. Her heart was melting with every action he took. She embraced her new journey into the heart of the French art of love-making.

He kissed Émilie tenderly and started to undress her. She trembled with excitement. It was not the first time that she was naked in front of him, but this magical moment made it very special. Her dress cascaded to the floor in front of the bath. Émilie was beautiful, gently curved, and toned. She looked like the Venus de Milo sculpture. Her flowing curls covered her perky, aroused breasts. She looked into Antoine with her big blue eyes. She was his. She was completely his.

ঞFrench Secretঞ

The French enjoy great love-making every day! They make it a priority in their relationship. The communion of the soul is a daily ritual. It strengthens the relationship. It brings fun and happiness and keeps the body's needs in balance. It's also a fantastic stress reliever.

Émilie and Antoine consummated their romance daily and discovered a little bit more about each other every chance they could. They embraced the French art of love-making with selfless attention towards each other. Antoine led Émilie in experimentation and helped her discover new ways to give and receive pleasure. Their daily "love bath" helped them relax and communicate with each other, strengthening their bond. Antoine spent the majority of his time on the radio with headquarters, getting information about the German retreat. It seemed that they were not going to use the escape route they expected. After two weeks of scouting, Lieutenant St. Germain received orders to leave the post, gather his troops, and join the Allies near Paris for a final push against the Germans.

Émilie noticed that Antoine seemed sad after his briefing with headquarters that morning.

"What happened, Antoine?" she asked, cuddling him from behind.

"We need to go soon. I am ordered to get my troops and join the Allies near Paris," Antoine muttered, lost in thought.

"So that means...." Émilie could not add another word. She needed time to process it all. She knew it meant the end was near. Their two weeks together in the farmhouse had been enchanting and she yearned for more. She wished they could stay this way forever. Her French officer was amazing in every way, and now he was going to be taken from her.

Antoine and Émilie packed the staff car and went back to the farm. The return trip was emotionally difficult. What can you say, what can you promise, when you know separation is inevitable? They were both deeply hurt. Their idyllic *séjour*, escaping the ravages of war, was ending. Antoine did not make any promises, and Émilie did not ask for a fairy tale ending. They assumed responsibility and both understood what the trip back to the farm meant. Instead of being sad, Émilie took this amazing experience as a blessing and soon after realized how many secrets had been revealed to her through the French art of love-making. It was a rapture that most people only dreamt of. The wishes she had made for years had finally come true. She had an extraordinary daily connection, deep affection, and true love.

Antoine and Émilie arrived at the farm close to dinner time. She was happy to see her family. Antoine's troops celebrated his return and were eager for information about the next mission. Cécile greeted Émilie with open arms. She had so much to tell her aunt about her adventure. After briefing his troops about the battle that was to be fought near Paris, the Lieutenant ordered them to prepare the artillery piece for the maneuvers. Émilie helped her officer prepare for his next mission, and then she cooked supper with Cécile for the men.

"Will you walk with me tonight, Antoine?" Émilie asked, hoping for one more taste of bliss.

"Of course. I would not miss this special moment for anything in the world," Antoine reassured her, smiling. All the while, he knew that this would be the last time they would make love to each other.

Later that evening, when everyone had gone their separate ways, Émilie grabbed her officer's hand. Without a word, they walked together and looked at the stars, as they did weeks before. A million candles filled the sky and led the way to the last chapter of their love story. When they arrived at their love rendezvous, Antoine laid out his beautiful blanket near the pond as he did the first night they made love. When he stood up, Émilie kissed him passionately.

This was a different Émilie. She was confident and led him in the French art of love-making. She undressed Antoine slowly. Love-making would be selfless that night, as it was every night. Pleasing each other with their tenderness, they experienced many blissful moments that they would both remember forever. After several hours of embracing and savoring one another, they gazed at the stars together for one last time.

Antoine knew the hour was late. Leading like the officer he was, Antoine blessed Émilie with one final passionate kiss. Helping her up, he took his blanket and folded it neatly. This *couverture d'amour* (love blanket) would soon become Lieutenant St. Germain's most valued possession. In the cold, lonely nights to come, this love blanket would bring him a smile and untouchable memories.

When they arrived back at the farm, Antoine embraced Émilie and said, "I need to check with my adjutant about the departure preparations."

"Yes, of course, Antoine," Émilie replied sadly. She turned and walked toward the house in silence.

She couldn't feel her feet on the cold rock pavement. Her pain was so overpowering that she was completely numb of all sensation. Tears abruptly began to flow down her face. Émilie tried to keep quiet. She didn't want to create a scene. When she entered the house, she immediately ran upstairs to her bedroom. Cécile and Renée gave Émilie space to process her immense pain. They had known this day was coming.

Heartbroken, Émilie retreated to her bedroom. She cried tears she had never cried before. This was a pain she had never known. She replayed the beautiful evenings she had spent with Antoine. She cuddled her goose down pillow. It was nothing like Antoine's body, but holding it helped her feel like it was. She had so many beautiful memories to cherish and share in her journal. She slowly drifted off to sleep, thinking of the wonderful times they had spent together.

Antoine finalized the preparations for their departure. Cécile, Renée, and several neighbors gathered to see them leave. Lieutenant St. Germain and his troops had been a blessing to their community. They helped them with daily tasks and eased the pain of war. They would be dearly missed.

Everything was in order except for one thing. Antoine needed to say his final goodbye to Émilie. He had dreaded this moment since the first time he saw Émilie.

Once more, showing his *chevaleresque* character, he went to see her. He climbed the stairs to Émilie's room. It was the only place he had never been with her alone. He opened the door to find her cuddling the large pillow. Émilie was asleep. Antoine brushed away a tear and smiled. Émilie looked like an angel. Seeing her beautiful long curly hair flowing over her perfect body was a picture that Antoine would remember forever. He approached her, making sure not to wake her up. In his hand, he held the final testament of his love. It was a note, rolled and inserted into his rose gold ring. The ring was a gift from Antoine's mother. She gave it to him the day he left for the front line. It was a ring that Lieutenant St. Germain had cherished for many years. He was now ready to pass it on. He was ready to give it to the only woman he had ever truly loved. He believed that, somehow, he could stay connected to her through this precious ring. Antoine took the note and placed it on Émilie's table. It would be the first thing she saw the next morning.

Now Antoine was ready to leave with his troops, under the cover of night. Led by the staff car, the convoy moved out. There was no celebration this time. Many soldiers held back their tears, while others could not. Cécile and Renée's farm was, for many of them, their closest memory of family.

The departure of the soldiers left the farm empty and silent. Cécile and Renée embraced each other for a while, as the sound of the convoy faded into the distance. Holding hands, they returned to the house. A glass of red wine and a piece of their finest cheese helped them sooth this painful departure.

The next morning was announced by a glorious sunrise. The farm had returned to normal life. Renée and Cécile were already out attending their *ménageries*. They had so much to do now that they were by themselves again.

Life on the farm was, once again, a little more difficult.

Émilie woke up facing a strange object on her night table. She immediately recognized Antoine's beautiful ring. She reached out and grabbed the scroll. Gently removing the ring and unrolling the note, she read the mysterious *parchemin* and began to cry once more. However, this time her tears stemmed from a different type pain. This overwhelming emotion towards him could only have meant one thing. Antoine was the love of her life and now he was gone. The only testament to this once-in-a-lifetime blessing was captured perfectly with his last note...

"Je t'aime..."

Émilie's Journal

Dear Journal,

I learned a valuable and exciting secret. After Antoine gave me his beautiful rose gold ring that I wear above my silver ring, I took some time to reflect on the French art of love-making. As my French officer taught me, there are three fundamental that reveal this secret. The first one is emotional intimacy (courting), then spiritual intimacy (romance), and finally physical intimacy (love-making).

Courting and the exercise of chivalry is the primary step to capture a person's heart. Antoine knew the importance of demonstrating his value and character in order to win my heart. He provided me with physical safety and a sense of emotional protection. He took time to establish trust and accepted my character fully. He demonstrated genuine kindness and empathy for my feelings, and proved to me that he had the qualities of a best friend.

Romance is where two souls give each other the gift of time to tighten the bonds of love. This is when, after I deemed him worthy of my love, I let him express his passion with light physical rapport. Kissing, caressing, and massaging signified his intention of protection, kindness, and closeness. It is also where our bond and connection formed deeply through constant, healthy communication. It was at that point that I truly tested Antoine's chevaleresque *character.*

Intimacy, or the French art of love-making, is about the culmination of all the subsequent parts, wrapped into action. It is a selfless expression of fulfilling your lover's needs. It is not about performing certain techniques or executing a sexual position. It is about taking the time to pleasure your love selflessly. It is about giving sexual satisfaction without expecting it in return. It's about being open to receiving the abundance of your lover.

ಐ

The Third Secret Ring

Communication, the Golden Key to the Soul of your Relationship

Communication, or the art of communicating effectively, in a relationship is crucial for French people—as it is for everyone! It is easy to picture the importance of communication by looking at any original French movie. Even a non-French-speaking person will understand the context of the film. Why? The French are extremely expressive. They use their entire body to share their message. They are also attentive in receiving the message properly. French is a difficult language to master. Therefore, a lot of emphasis is added in using the whole body in order to properly communicate and be understood.

The third secret to love and happiness is the ability to communicate effectively in your relationship.

Without mastering this skill, you will run into arguments caused by miscommunication. We will learn this skill through Émilie's story, which will help you master healthy communication skills that will completely transform your relationship.

ೞ

Mid-July 1944 was exceptionally warm in Limoges. Émilie heard that the Germans and Allies were battling in northern France, Normandy. The war would soon be over for France. Émilie was overjoyed to think that she and Antoine would be reunited for good.

"I really hope he's okay. I can't believe I haven't received a letter from him for so long," thought Émilie, saddened.

By that time, it had been five weeks since she'd received any correspondence from Antoine. She was frustrated and worried. Émilie thought her beautiful dream was over.

Émilie used to receive a letter from him every single day. He wrote about how much he loved her and how wonderful she was. He wrote that he could not wait for the war to end so they could be together, forever. He made sure not to write about the atrocities he witnessed. Instead, he kept it light so she would not worry. Limiting the information in his letters was his way of protecting her. Antoine was made of integrity, and his word was his badge of honor. Émilie knew that. In her mind, the fact that he had broken his promise to write every day until they reunited was a sure sign that something had happened. She tried to rationalize the situation but could not bury her feelings of distress.

The lack of communication was driving her crazy. "I will find him!" Émilie said to herself with determination. "I remember him talking on the radio to his headquarters about a small village near Paris. Créteil was the name, I think," she recalled. "I need to find him. I need to be with him. The war is almost over and I want nothing to get in the way of my love for him. I must go at once. I am sure Aunty will understand."

Émilie and Cecile had a heart-to-heart conversation that night. Cecile tried to convince her to stay until the Germans surrendered Paris, but Émilie could not bear the thought of being separated from her love for one more minute. Cécile understood and agreed to take her to the train station the next morning.

It was 6:40 a.m. The Limoges train station was empty. The sun fought to peak through a canopy of grey clouds. The air was fresh and moist. Cécile and Émilie waited together at the station. Soon enough a large plume of dark smoke rose in the distance, followed by a whistle. It was the signal of the beginning of yet another new adventure for Émilie. They stood together holding hands. Neither one wanted to break this special moment.

Cécile remembered waiting for a train to take her away on an adventure as well... long ago. Today it was her niece's turn. The train pulled in front of them. It was strange. July was typically busy at this train station. It was summer vacation season. Parents and children, along with their pets, would travel during their time off. It was not uncommon for people to spend four months in the south. St. Tropez and Nice were the popular destinations. These days were different. Times of uncertainty raised fear and brought caution to people's hearts.

However, Émilie did not feel any fear. She was single-minded and in love. The word *impossible* did not exist to her. Thanks to self-love, her personal power was strong and predominant.

"It's time, Aunty," Émilie said with mixed emotions.

Cécile simply kissed her on the forehead and gave her few words of advice. "I trust you, Émilie. Remember that I love you. I love you like my own daughter."

Émilie smiled, picked up her leather bag, and stepped onto the train. She remembered the last time she was on a train. Antoine had been there to hold her hand. The tender image filled her heart with courage and determination. She missed his love. She missed her only love. She missed the man who taught her the French art of love-making. She was craving his strong, tender, masculine support. Everything was so easy when Antoine was around.

The train slowly departed toward Créteil, without a whistle this time. Émilie blew many kisses to Cécile through the window. Her aunt pretended to catch them all. Émilie felt loved, understood, and supported. This adventure was like nothing she had experienced before. This time she didn't know exactly where she was heading, but it made the trip that much more exciting.

Once more, she found that no one was in her assigned cabin. It was hot and steamy. Créteil was three hours and thirty minutes away. The train wouldn't stop as frequently for identity checks. This time, the Germans had more important things to do.

"I wonder what Antoine is doing. I really hope that he's still in Créteil," Émilie thought with a creeping sense of doubt.

The train advanced as planned. Émilie took the time to enter a few comments in her personal journal, which was almost filled now. She had been diligently writing every day. Writing was one of her passions. She gave herself this special time to regroup and recollect. Practicing self-love every day was one of her favorite activities. It gave her a grounding perspective of who she really was.

After writing for some time, she paused to check her watch. It was 9:13 a.m.

"Only one more hour before another adventure begins."

She closed her eyes and tried to get some rest before her arrival. She wanted to imagine her reunion with Antoine. She wanted to dream of long, passionate kisses. She wanted to dream of a future forever, but as hard as she tried, she could not make her dreams appear in the hot, steamy cabin. It flustered her. She had experienced so many new things and so many passionate moments with Antoine. She could not wait to be in his arms once more. She wanted to be taken, mind, body, and soul.

The time was drawing near. Émilie felt the train begin to slow down. Through the speakers, the conductor announced that they would arrive in ten minutes. She placed her journal back into her leather bag and took a quick bite of cheese and baguette that Cécile had given her that morning. Everything was fresh. She also had a bottle of milk and some wine from the farm. Her hope was to have the first glass with Antoine upon their reunion.

Émilie looked out the window to get herself familiarized with the surroundings. Créteil was similar to Limoges, however the people seemed to be happier. Possibly it was the knowledge that the war was coming to an end and Paris would soon be free. She could sense the winds of change. The city was only twelve kilometers from *centre de Paris*, and only three hours from where the Allies were invading Normandy. Créteil would be the city the Germans passed through when they retreated from Paris to Germany. That was the reason Antoine and the French Resistance assembled there. They were there to delay their retreat.

The train finally came to a halt. It was raining but there were many people waiting at the station. The atmosphere was animated. There were no Germans that she could see, and everyone seemed somewhat liberated. Émilie took her suitcase and leather backpack, and set foot on the wet pavement. She looked around to get her sense of direction.

What now? she thought, walking out of the station through the people entering and exiting, she noticed a man in a strange military uniform. It was neither German nor French.

"Perhaps he's American or British," she speculated. "Maybe he knows where the French Resistance Regiment is."

The man was by himself, smoking a cigarette and looking at something across the street. Émilie was a little frightened, but her motto was "fortune favors the brave" so she approached the tall man.

"Good day, dear sir," Émilie said in a respectful voice.

The man turned to look at her. He had pale blue eyes and a moustache that curled upward on both sides. He looked peculiar, but there was a sense of calmness in him that reassured Émilie.

"Good day, my dear. What can I do for you?" the man answered in a strong British accent.

She knew, for sure now, that he was not a German. "I was wondering if you could help me find someone," Émilie asked shyly.

"It depends if this person is familiar to me," said the man, gave a half-grin and revealing a gold tooth. "Let me introduce myself. I am Captain Sir John MacAllester. I am a pastor attached to the British

Airborne Regiment," he declared with a clear sense of pride in his voice.

"I am Émilie Durant from St. Girons. I'm here to find my friend Antoine St. Germain. He is a Lieutenant with the French Resistance," Émilie replied, hoping the man knew him.

"The French Resistance is everywhere. Unless he is in uniform he will be difficult to find. However, we have received orders to liaise with a French Artillery Regiment later this week. Maybe they know him," John suggested.

"You are a pastor with the Airborne Regiment?" Émilie inquired, a bit surprised.

"Yes! And the cook as well," John roared with a belly laugh. "I was a pastor in Yorkshire, England before this bloody war started. I wanted to bring God to the men who needed it most," he continued with a sense of purpose in his voice.

John was a great pastor in his church. He was well loved and respected. Both the old and young sought him out to speak with him. John was an expert in the art of communication. He knew how to listen and be there at the exact moment anyone needed his advice. Being a man of God, he tried to follow God's command. Above all, he never used the four sins of communication.

Émilie had never met someone with such a sense of purpose. John had a special way of communicating. He could open the hearts and minds of people. Émilie would soon find out his secret, the third secret of love and happiness, the golden key to the soul of any relationship.

Émilie was happy to think that she might find Antoine soon. It couldn't be soon enough. John could see her obvious disappointment.

"Émilie, I may be able to help you to find your friend," said John in a compassionate voice. "St. Christophe church is a stronghold for the French Resistance. Pastor David is a good friend of mine and connected to the Resistance. Perhaps he can help you," John comforted her.

"That would be wonderful," Émilie exclaimed.

"I can bring you there as soon as my deputy commander finishes his meeting. He's across the street dealing with some reconnaissance information," John explained, pointing at the building across the street.

"Very well. Would you like something to eat or drink? My aunty gave me a nice piece of cheese and a baguette this morning. I also have a bottle of milk and some wine if you would like," Émilie offered in an attempt to return the favour.

"Thank you for the generous offer, Émilie. I am fine for now. Some villagers gave us food and water this morning," replied John with a genuine tone of thankfulness. "Oh, I see Major Cavendish coming our way."

The Major dashed across the street to Émilie and John.

"So how was it?" John inquired.

"Great news! I think it's the beginning of the end. The Allies are inland with more supplies than ever. The Yanks sure know how to throw their weight around, God bless them," spouted Major Cavendish. "Who is this young lady, John?" he asked.

"This is Émilie Durant from St-Girons. She is here to find her friend, Lieutenant Antoine St. Germain of the French Resistance," John answered.

"I think I heard of this young lieutenant two days ago," the Major recalled, rubbing his chin.

Émilie beamed like a ray of sunlight when she heard the news. "You've heard of Antoine?" she buzzed.

"Yes, but I haven't heard about him since. He seems to be quite a courageous lad," the Major continued.

"How so?" asked John.

"The last message we received about him was spectacular. He had taken three hundred and forty-one prisoners with only twenty-one men with him," recounted the Major, raising an eyebrow.

Émilie could picture Antoine performing such a fantastic act of valor. However, she still didn't understand why he stopped writing to her. She was proud of him, but disappointed at the same time. A new feeling was starting to surface. She had lost some of her admiration for him. She started to feel resentment and doubt about their future together. Was it possible that Antoine had lied or prioritized his need to fight over his need to love and be loved by her? All of these thoughts started to weigh on Émilie. Her perception of Antoine, and perhaps even her love for him, hung in the balance. She tried to push these feelings away. It was, after all, the greatest battle that France had ever faced. Her wants and needs had to be on hold for now.

ᛇFrench Secretᛇ

Communication is at the heart of all healthy relationships. Any feelings related to vengeance, judgment, criticism, and aggression will damage your relationship for certain.

"Major, I was wondering if we could bring our friend to the St. Christophe Church. I know the pastor well and he could certainly know where this young lieutenant is," John requested.

"Very well, we are close by anyway. A friend of a hero is a friend of ours. Isn't that right, Captain?" said the Major, looking at John.

"I wholeheartedly agree, Major," John concurred.

They climbed into the staff car. The Major opened the door for Émilie while John slipped behind the wheel.

"Thank you, Major," she said in appreciation.

The staff car started without hesitation. John drove slowly up the street and turned left on *la rue Paul-François*. The trip took twenty minutes. During the trip, they spoke about their past and current lives with Émilie. She recognized a lot of the same characteristics that Antoine had. The military life had a special way in developing integrity in a person. As they chatted about their dreams, the St. Christophe Church appeared in front of them.

The church was magnificent. It was built in the 12th century and sat at the very center of Créteil. They drove around the church and stopped at the side of the building. Only John and Émilie stepped out of the vehicle.

"Come with me, Émilie," John said. "I will ask Pastor David if he is able to offer a place for you to stay for a little while."

"Thank you very much for this generous offer, Captain," Émilie smiled, quite touched.

When they entered the church, light beamed onto them through the stained glass. The church was serene. Only sunlight and candles lit the inside. A strong smell of incense filled God's palace. The paintings inside were centuries old. A sense of peace and calmness surrounded the entire premise. Pastor David was praying from the second row of benches. John and Émilie approached him after paying respect to God. Hearing their footsteps, Pastor David turned around and beamed a delighted smile at the sight of his old friend. Pastor David had been a man of the church since he was a young boy, but now white hair covered his head and the lower half of his face. He had devoted his life to the love of God and to spreading his message to his fellow *paroissian* (parishioners). He gave courage and faith to those in need. He gave comfort to the ones who sought him. Pastor David was a man you could trust.

"Good day, my friends," said Pastor David in an enthused and cheerful voice. "It's really nice to see you again, John," he added.

"Good day, David. It is nice to see you. You seem as if you are doing well," John noted.

"I am not sure about that but I'm living in peace for certain. Who have you brought with you?" Pastor David inquired.

"This is Émilie Durant, from St-Girons. She is here to find her friend, Antoine St. Germain. He's a young lieutenant in the French Resistance. Have you heard of him?" John inquired, hoping to make Émilie's dreams come true.

"I don't believe so. Many young men come and go these days. It's a real shame to see this. Perhaps my assistant, Suzanne, has heard of him," Pastor David offered up in a tone that was not the most reassuring.

"Thank you very much, Pastor David. I would really like to talk to Suzanne when she's available," Émilie said hopefully.

"I was wondering if you could provide shelter and food for our new friend," John asked.

"Of course. We have plenty of room. I am sure Émilie will be comfortable with us," Pastor David assured them.

"Perhaps I could provide assistance to Suzanne while I'm here," Émilie offered, wishing not to be a burden.

"I'm sure Suzanne would appreciate your help," the pastor affirmed.

"Then it's settled. I will come see you tomorrow, Émilie. I want to know if you hear word of your friend," John said emphatically.

"I would love that, Captain. Thank you so very much," Émilie said, feeling truly blessed from all the generosity she was receiving.

Émilie took her suitcase and followed Pastor David to the church house. While walking, Pastor David heard Émilie talking to herself. He heard criticisms and disrespectful comments about her friend, Antoine. David knew about the four sins of communication.

The pastor stopped and turned around to look at Émilie. "My dear child, I couldn't help but hear you talking to yourself about your friend," he said in a concerned tone.

"Antoine? Yes. I came all the way here to find him. I am not even sure if he wants to be with me," Émilie spat harshly.

"You have to give him the benefit of the doubt, Émilie. I am sure he is thinking of you, but right now he has his duty to fulfill," Pastor David advised her.

"I apologize, Pastor David, but I am feeling resentment and bitterness. I'm trying to forgive him and let it go, but it doesn't seem to be working," Émilie admitted.

"Resentment and frustration are the breeding grounds of dark emotions. They turn your heart black and your words to poison," Pastor David explained.

Émilie looked down in shame and was quiet for the remainder of their walk to the rectory.

ಶFrench Secretಶ

Resentment is by far the number one enemy of any relationship. This emotion can destroy any good memories that you may have had with your love.

When they finally arrived, Émilie saw that the house was nicely decorated and smelled fresh. A scent of French lavender filled the air.

"You can put your suitcase here, Émilie. Suzanne will help you with the rest. Are you hungry?" asked Pastor David.

"I am fine for now. I will wait until supper," Émilie replied.

"Very well. You will have to excuse me for now. I need to prepare for this evening's mass," declared the Pastor.

"Thank you for everything. I'm so very grateful for what you are doing for me," Émilie said with a clear tone of appreciation.

"May God give you strength and clarity," prayed David as he blessed Émilie with the sign of the cross.

She could not speak. Émilie did not know what to think. She'd felt strong, determined, and courageous since embarking on her journey, and she couldn't understand what the Pastor saw in her that needed strength and clarity.

Émilie sat outside on the porch while she waited for Suzanne, Pastor David's blessing still resonating in her soul. Soon a woman emerged from the church with a basket full of fresh vegetables. That must be Suzanne, Émilie thought. The young woman waved at Émilie and offered a friendly smile.

Émilie felt immediately welcomed by her. Walking with sure steps, the woman stopped to pick some flowers that were growing beside the fence that encircled the church house.

"*Bonjour, Émilie*," Suzanne sang.

Arriving at the steps, she climbed them quickly and gave Émilie a kiss on both cheeks. Now Émilie felt very welcome. So much love and support had been blessed upon her.

"I am Suzanne, Pastor David's assistant. He told me about your gracious visit a few minutes ago. He also told me that you were looking for your friend, Antoine," Suzanne continued, barely holding her enthusiasm.

"Yes, that's right. I am very pleased to meet you, Suzanne," echoed Émilie with a big smile. "I came all the way from Limoges to find him. He is a lieutenant in the French Resistance. He mentioned that he would be in Créteil with his platoon. His name is Antoine St. Germain. Have you heard of him?" Émilie asked, hoping for a positive answer.

"Hmm. This name sounds familiar but I will have to ask around," Suzanne answered.

Émilie's stomach sank. It was not the response she was hoping for. Once again, frustration and resentment filled her heart. She could not help it.

"You look sad, Émilie," Suzanne noted with concern on her face.

"I am—and extremely bitter towards him," Émilie said flatly, trying to hold her anger.

"I am also waiting for my fiancée. He is an American Airborne of the Screaming Eagle Regiment," said Suzanne.

"How did you meet?" Émilie asked.

"It's a long story. We can talk about it after supper," Suzanne offered with a smile.

Émilie helped Suzanne bring the vegetables inside the rectory and closed the door behind her.

They passed the afternoon exchanging stories and doing chores around the church. They talked about where they grew up, their families, friends, and dreams. Suzanne was an excellent communicator. However, her self-love needed some help. Suzanne practiced self-responsibility. She fully accepted what was happening in her life and understood that she created her current reality for herself. Unfortunately, her self-affirmation was non-existent. Suzanne put herself down regularly when she spoke. Émilie noticed this and did not understand. Suzanne was amazing at everything she put her heart into. Émilie felt sad for her. She believed that her self-love would never be complete without self-affirmation, so she decided to help her.

Later that day, Suzanne and Émilie were getting along very well. They had a lot in common. They seemed to embrace *une amitiée durable* (best friend qualities). These were the same qualities that Michelle had talked about. They made dinner together and enjoyed a conversation with Pastor David. However, every time Émilie talked about Antoine, her heart darkened and her words became poison towards him. It was not normal for Émilie to speak this way. She just couldn't help it.

After supper, Émilie asked if John had confirmed his visit with her for the next day. The pastor was not sure. He had not heard back from him. Émilie hoped for a surprise visit. She liked the way that he made her feel secure and calm.

Night fell upon Créteil. Suzanne and Émilie went upstairs. They both had a full day ahead of them. Émilie wanted to make sure that she was contributing. She did not want to be a burden on Pastor David or Suzanne. Their kindness and open hearts set the perfect conditions for Émilie to receive her third secret of love and happiness.

౿*French Secret*౿

Stay connected. Feed each other's souls.

The next morning blossomed with beautiful sunshine. The air was fresh and the scent of lavender entered the house on a warm breeze from the south. Sunlight penetrated the first floor through the windows like a personal gift from above. It seemed as if time was standing still. Émilie took in the beautiful surroundings. The kitchen and eating areas were filled with food storage. Cured cheese, salami, dried meats, vegetables, fruits, and cans of food covered the walls. The aroma was enchanting. Émilie wondered why there was so much food around. It must be there for a reason. She had never seen anything like this before.

Émilie went to the stove and lit the iron "monster". She wanted to surprise Pastor David and Suzanne. She fetched some eggs and potatoes. Her plan was to prepare omelets for her kind benefactors. Soon enough, the sizzle and smell of breakfast woke up the Pastor and Suzanne. She could hear the floor creaking from above. Suzanne was the first to come down.

"Émilie, what are you doing?" she asked, barely awake.

"I'm preparing breakfast for the Pastor and you," Émilie replied.

"Wonderful. Thank you so much. I can't remember the last time someone made breakfast for me. The Pastor will love this treat as well. He's always too busy for breakfast, with his *paroissian* asking for his help," Suzanne added.

"What do you mean, Suzanne?" Émilie asked.

"All this food will be shared with people in need. Then, after four o'clock, merchants will come and deliver some more vegetables and products," Suzanne said proudly. "Around here they call Pastor David 'Saint David'".

"Incredible. That's why there is so much food everywhere," Émilie noted, taken aback.

"This isn't all. There's more in the cold cellar," she boasted.

Pastor David peeked his nose over the banister. "My Lord, my dear Lord, what is that wonderful smell?" he asked.

"Émilie prepared breakfast for us, Pastor," Suzanne replied loudly.

"Well then, I'll be down shortly," Pastor David chirped, obviously enthused.

Suzanne told Émilie that Pastor David always said his prayers before coming downstairs. It was his way of thanking the Lord for all the beautiful things He had provided and for His ability to help so many people around him. Émilie was deeply touched by the sense of purpose in the church house. She recognized the self-appreciation they possessed.

Pastor David came downstairs humming a song.

"You seem happy, Pastor," Suzanne commented with a smile.

"Of course. I am so blessed to have two wonderful helpers with me. Have any of our *paroissian* come yet this morning?" he asked.

"No, I haven't seen anyone yet," Émilie replied to the pastor. "I made omelets and sliced fried potatoes," she continued.

"Fantastic!" David exclaimed.

Everyone was happy. The day could not have begun better. It was the first time Émilie had not thought about Antoine in some time. She felt blessed to have found such supportive new friends.

Pastor David needed help painting the chapel. Émilie volunteered for the task, while Suzanne remained at the church house to distribute food to the ones in need.

After doing the morning dishes, Émilie busied herself painting the small chapel at the back of the church. It had been used many years before to lodge some of the *paroissien* whose houses had burnt down.

She was lost in thought when she noticed a green army jeep coming towards the house. She immediately recognized Captain John with his funny moustache. The captain waved at her and smiled. She happily rushed out to greet him.

"Good day, John. I was really hoping you would come and see me today," said Émilie, enthused.

"Of course. I promised, remember?" John declared with integrity. "How are Suzanne and Pastor David?" he asked.

"Wonderful. They told me that I could stay here for a little while. Until I find Antoine, I guess," she said hopefully.

The Four Secret Rings of Love and Happiness

"On that subject, I asked around at the headquarters and found out nothing on Lieutenant St. Germain. There have been no reports about him over the HQ radio. He must have moved closer to Paris. The Germans are on the run. The French Resistance is really making a difference with their sabotage operations," related John, hoping that Émilie would not get upset with the news.

Émilie fell to her knees. "That's it. That's it. He lied to me. I don't want to hear anything about him anymore," she cried.

"Émilie, I understand your sadness and frustration but I feel your heart is darkening. You are also using the *péchés mortelles* (deadly sin) of communication. This does not help you with what is happening here," John said empathically, kneeling by her side.

Émilie raised her head, tears flowing down her cheek. Captain John took his handkerchief and dried it for her. Émilie was touched by his kindness.

She looked at him, disillusioned. "What do you mean by *péchés mortelles* of communication? I communicate very well," Émilie insisted.

"I noticed yesterday that you use poison words to describe your friend, Antoine. From the report that we received about him, he is a very courageous young man. You really have to give him the benefit of the doubt. Émilie, we are at war, and Lieutenant

St. Germain is a brave and courageous soldier. I am convinced that he thinks of you every day because you are an incredible person. But for now, circumstances are preventing him from sharing his love with you," said Captain John, compassionately. He added, "How do you think he would feel if he was in front of you when you used such words?" John asked politely, trying not to hurt Émilie's ego.
"He would probably feel hurt like I do right now," Émilie replied in anger.

"Is it the goal to hurt him or to express your feelings of hurt? The majority of people confuse or ignore the essence of communication, which is to simply convey or relay a message or feeling from one mind to another. Anything more than that obstructs the message. The simpler the message, the clearer and easier it is to understand. Clear communication, the ability to listen and speak well, is one of the fundamentals of a happy relationship," John explained.

Émilie looked puzzled. She wanted to understand, and she knew that the Captain was saying something important. However, Émilie was too upset to grasp the information. Captain John knew that, too.

"Let me help you paint the chapel for a while, Émilie. I have about twenty minutes before I need to go. I will be back tomorrow to teach about the *péchés mortelles* and my secret for effectively communicating emotions and thoughts. I will also teach you how to listen and understand what someone is trying to tell you. I use it all the time with couples in my parish. The results are remarkable. It has saved many relationships and marriages," asserted the captain with a clear tone of pride in his voice. "The first thing I teach couples that come to see me for advice is the need to forbid the use of the four *péchés mortelle*. The minute you use them, you poison your words and the message you are trying to convey. I will tell you tomorrow how this poison affects the person you are trying communicate with," Captain John affirmed with a nod.

༺*French Secret*༻

The four péchés mortelles *of communication can ruin any well-intended message. It is imperative that you try, at all costs, to stay clear of them. Realizing the impact of their use will make you stop using them altogether.*

Émilie nodded. Captain John took Émilie's arm and helped her up. He took the paintbrushes and bucket, and they both continued to paint the chapel without speaking.

These moments were precious. Émilie was pensive, reflecting on what John had just told her. She remembered that her mother, Michelle, had made a few attempts to explain the importance of communicating effectively on her self-improvement journey. Émilie was, at times, quick to judge and criticize. She knew she had hurt many people around her in the past. She was ashamed and recognized her responsibility in her current situation. She began to think that maybe Antoine had been patient with her communication style. She realized that she needed help with her ability to listen and communicate. At that moment, she decided to make a note in her journal about assuming responsibility for the way she communicated with others. It would become her new goal: giving the gift of communication!

Soon it was time for John to leave. Émilie appreciated the message of compassion he had given her.

"I will be back tomorrow, Émilie," Captain John promised.

"Yes, please. I can't wait to learn more about communication," Émilie smiled.

John turned his jeep around and they waved to one another as he drove off.

It wasn't long before the chapel renovations were complete. Émilie decided to take a break and see what Suzanne and Pastor David were doing. She heard a lot of happy chatter coming from the house as she put away the brushes and paint near the wall of the church.

Many people came in and out of the rectory. Émilie

noticed that everyone entering had sadness on their faces, but when they came out, it was a different story. Every single person was filled with joy and happiness. It was like a miracle. Maybe it was the miracle of God's love in action.

ஐ*French Secret*ஐ

Greeting, for the French, is crucial. It is their way to say "I welcome you with love and an open heart".

"Bonjour, Émilie," said Suzanne seeing her enter with some of the *paroissien*. She was portioning food for some people who had lined up. Everyone seemed to know her. They discussed their problems and helped each other by exchanging services such as house and farm maintenance. Suzanne was the *grand chef d'orchestre* (conductor of the orchestra).

"Émilie, could you please help Madame Laliberté, with her bags?

The old French woman looked at Émilie with gratitude and the purest smile. Before leaving, Madame Laliberté whispered a few words in Émilie's ear. "You will never be alone. You have a the Gift of the Golden Heart! Pursue the righteous path of love."

Émilie's heart almost stopped. She spoke so much truth in so few words. It felt like a divine prophecy.

Then, Madame Laliberté simply turned around and walked away.

ᛤ*French Secret*ᛤ

The French always have a sense of communion with each other. Their strong pride in their heritage and language has made them what they are today.

Émilie could not stop thinking about what Madame Laliberté had said to her.

That evening, she asked Suzanne about her. "Do you know the old lady that I was talking to?"

Suzanne gave Émilie a sideways glance, "She looked through your soul, didn't she?"

"How did you know?" Émilie asked, stunned.

"Madame Laliberté is a very special woman. Many people around here call her *la femme sage* (the wise woman). She never communicates more than she needs to and always praises the people around her who deserve it. Madame Laliberté is a wise woman, indeed. She lost her husband in the Great War and never remarried. Instead, she married her community and helps anyone in need," Suzanne whispered.

They both sat in silence for a minute.

"I want to be wise like her," Émilie blurted out.

"You are in so many ways, Émilie. You have only been here a few days and you're already making a difference in my life and the lives of the *paroissien*, Suzanne assured her.

"*Merci*, Suzanne. I want to give the best to everyone around me," Émilie said.

"Don't we all," Suzanne agreed.

That evening Émilie, Suzanne, and Pastor David played cards. Laughter and joy filled the provision-packed kitchen. They lived in a world of abundance, yet the act of giving was the most important aspect of it all. Émilie was overjoyed with the riches of self-appreciation. Later that night, she spent an hour collecting her thoughts on the day and recorded them in her journal.

The next morning, Émilie waited for Captain John impatiently. Her conversation with Suzanne and Pastor David had opened her mind and heart to the beautiful gift of healthy communication. It was already 10:05 a.m. and Émilie was busy helping Suzanne with the *paroissien* when she caught a glimpse of the green army jeep coming up the drive. She was excited and happy that today was to be the day she would begin to learn and understand healthy communication skills.

Captain John waved to her. Émilie scurried outside to greet the Captain as he climbed out of his jeep. He had a beautiful leather-bound book with him.

She wondered what the book could possibly be.

They greeted each other with a kiss on both cheeks.

"How are you, Émilie?" Captain John asked.

"I'm fantastic. I have to admit that I am very happy and appreciate that you are spending this time with me. I didn't realize that I needed help with the way I communicate and the way I listen," Émilie stated, inspired.

John smiled and handed her the leather-bound book.

"For me?" asked Émilie, surprised and touched.

"Yes, it is. I have had this notebook with me for a long time. I brought it from England, hoping that one day I would use it to write my wartime memoirs. However, after yesterday, I think it would be more meaningful for you to record your journey towards the gift of communication," Captain John stated matter-of-factly. "Are you ready to learn?" he asked.

"Yes, and I will write down your teachings in the notebook," Émilie said happily.

"Very well. Let's sit under the tree over there," John suggested, guiding Émilie to a large oak near the pathway that lead to the church.

They both sat down. Émilie opened her new notebook and looked attentively at Captain John.

"Émilie, I will teach you a very important and valuable skill that will be with you for the rest of your life. I hope you will pass this secret on to many people around you," he began.
"Yes, of course," Émilie nodded, eyes wide.

"I was taught this secret many years ago and have taught this impressive method to hundreds of couples in my diocese. All of them, without exception, have saved a failing relationship and replaced it for one of love and happiness," John said, obviously proud of his results.

Émilie was impressed and could not wait to hear more.

John continued. "Relationships are very much like a beautiful grape vine. If you take care of them, they will give you the best wine. However, if you neglect to provide the essentials, they need they will produce raisins, or get parasites, or simply die.

"Communication in a relationship is crucial. You must apply it carefully and regularly," John explained.

Émilie captured every single word, and then looked at Captain John. "It sounds like a lot of work," she said.

"Not at all. It becomes like second nature in time."
Émilie sighed in relief and they both laughed.

"It always surprises me to see how many couples talk to each other without really listening or understanding the essence of what is being said. Both people must be available physically, spiritually, and emotionally to share and receive conversation with an open mind and open heart. I always remind myself before every important discussion that I have made a PACT with communication."

Émilie looked puzzled and asked, "Can you tell me more about the pact you made?"

John smiled, happy that she asked. "I am glad you asked. You must be willing and able to communicate responsibly and truly appreciate the gift of communication.

"I always think of the PACT that I made to others and loved ones by starting every critical communication with the following acronym."

John took Émilie's notebook and wrote the following:

(P)reparation.

(A)ct and express my message emphatically, then I

(C)onclude or summarize my understanding of the outcome and always say

(T)hank you.

"This way of communicating has an additional benefit or result: *Togetherness.*
"When you communicate effectively, the relationship with your loved one will strengthen and mature. You will feel closer than ever. The problem with the way most people communicate is that they are not aware of the PACT. They communicate using their normal way of expressing themselves. You know, the exchange of information where the message is mostly factual," said John, looking to Émilie for a reply.

"Yes, I know what you mean," she agreed. "Every time I get upset about something, I blurt out the first thing that comes to mind without thinking it through. It's usually a judgment or critical comments." She continued. "Now I know what I've done wrong and will assume full responsibility for the problems in my relationships, particularly with Antoine. I humbly recognize that, at times, I was not the most sympathetic toward him or his need to be understood. Some of my letters to Antoine were judgmental and selfish. Perhaps that is why he…" She looked down, ashamed, incapable of finishing her sentence. She suddenly realized the impact of poor communication skills in a relationship.

"Émilie. Most, if not all, of the couples that need my help communicate emotional messages the same way you have and suffer the same relationship problems. Using the sins of communication destroys the love that your partner has for you, bit by bit. It creates the perfect ground for resentment and revenge. It bruises egos. None of these things nourish love and happiness." John stopped for a moment for Émilie to understand his important teaching.

"Could you tell me a little more about the sins of communication?" asked Émilie, turning to a new page of her notebook.

John smiled and continued. "When the four sins of communication are used by either the listener or the speaker, the conversation is poisoned and doomed to fail," said John said with authority and from experience. "I think it's time to review the *quatre péchés mortelles*. I have a sermon that I used to read every last Sunday of the month. It's about the danger of using these *fléaux* (atrocities) in any of your relationships. I've seen more marriages and relationships destroyed by these terrible acts than I care to remember," John stated with emotion in his voice.

Émilie was now extremely anxious to learn about them so she would never use them again.

Captain John taught on. "You must stay away from being *critique* (critical), *mépris* (disrespectful), *muraille* (defensive) and *larguer* (disengaged). These are the four communication killers that will destroy any well intended discussion." She looked at the list and reviewed them mentally. The area in which she needed the most help was now evident.

Émilie and John continued to chat about the gift of communication and its immense benefits but Émilie was becoming a bit overwhelmed, to say the least.

She remembered that her mother, Michelle, had always been attentive to her when she came for advice. She always allowed her to share her thoughts. She would always summarize Émilie's message, which made her feel special and understood. Above all else, she remembered that her mother never used any of the four sins of communication. Émilie now realized why she always felt welcome to share anything with her.

All this new knowledge about communication and the impact that it had on the people surrounding her made Émilie realize how she had negatively impacted her relationship with Antoine.

"Now I will be able to provide the gift of understanding and openness to people around me," said Émilie, looking at Captain John with satisfaction.

John was taken aback. He knew that Émilie came into his life for a reason. Being a pastor, he had seen many miracles. This was one of them. Knowing that the gift of communication would be shared with Émilie's acquaintances counted as his blessing for the day.

Captain John looked at Émilie humbly and said, "And this is my secret delivered to you, Émilie."
"How can I ever repay you for this amazing gift?" Émilie pleaded.
"Use your new knowledge anytime you have a chance and remember the PACT that you made with communication. It will provide you and others with something fantastic. It's a gift that few people have ever received: the gift of being truly understood," John assured her.

It was getting late and John had to leave again. It would be the last time Émilie ever saw him. The Allies' advance to Paris was eminent, and many lives would be changed forever. The Airborne Regiment was to take a bridge near Paris and block the German's retreat.

John and Émilie had spent the whole afternoon talking about this beautiful gift. Émilie read over her notes and reflected her understanding back to him. She had captured the essence that would enable her to help others now.

"I must go, Émilie," said Captain John.

"Will I see you tomorrow?" Émilie asked hopefully.

"No. My work is done here," John replied, giving her his hallmark half-smile. Émilie understood. John had come into her life for a single purpose, to give her the third secret of love and happiness, the gift of communication.

They stood up together, and Émilie hugged Captain John tightly and thanked him for his time and generosity. John was touched by Émilie's kind heart. Her openness and gentle soul moved him. He looked down at his hand and took off the ring that was on his little finger. It had a bronze finish, and wine branches and leaves weaving around it. The ring was extremely special to John. It represented humbleness in power and giving back to others. Taking Émilie's hand, he put it on her right index finger.

"Here, Émilie, a small gift to help you remember to share the gift of communication. My mentor and good friend, Pastor Paul, gave it to me back in England many years ago. He gave me this ring the day I finally understood the miracle of communication and the healing it provides to troubled souls. Now I would like for you to wear and honor it. You are ready," he said softly.

"I will take great care of it and cherish it forever. I will remind myself every day of my blessings and give the gift of understanding," Émilie promised with genuine truth in her eyes.

John hugged Émilie one final time then turned and got into his jeep. Émilie didn't know his next mission but she was certain that he would make a difference. He already had in her life. Goodness always rises above evil.

Émilie returned to the church house to help Suzanne with supper. She was pensive but finally at peace with Antoine, as she accepted responsibility for her current situation with him. She also understood that he had other priorities beyond her, but above all else, her unhealthy communication style had probably ruined their relationship.

ҨFrench SecretҨ

Beware of your communication style with your loved one. You have the power to bring fortune or disaster into their lives.

Give the gift of communication

Once Émilie arrived at the church, Suzanne greeted her cheerfully. Émilie needed that. She had become an amazing friend by demonstrating all the elements of an *amitiée durable*. Suzanne did not ask what happened with John. However she did notice the third ring on her finger.

"Is that a gift from Captain John?" asked Suzanne.

"Yes, a kind and selfless offering. It reminds me of my new blessing. The gift of communication," said Émilie, toying with her new ring.

Suzanne was lost for words. She was, herself, a great communicator, and knew that this gift was a valuable and life changing one.

Émilie stayed with Pastor David and Suzanne a few more weeks. Every day, she helped them deliver food to those in need. However, something unusual started to happen. More and more people began coming to the rectory, not to receive food but to talk to Émilie. They had taken more comfort in her gift of connecting with their souls than the food they could take with them. They often went for walks with her in the park adjacent to the church, where it was peaceful. Everyone shared the same feeling when they returned: enlightenment and peace.

On Friday, August 25th, 1944, Émilie was preparing breakfast when Suzanne arrived at the rectory out of breath. She was noticeably moved by some news she heard at the market that morning.

"The Germans surrendered Paris!" she shouted.

Émilie and Suzanne opened a bottle of wine to celebrate. It would be cabernet sauvignon and crêpes that morning. Pastor David came running downstairs when he heard the news, forgetting his prayers for the moment. The war would be over soon.

Suzanne also heard that the 8th U.S. Army was planning a march down *avenue des Champs-Elysées* that coming Tuesday, August 29th. They had to go. They had to go celebrate in Paris. They asked Pastor David for his blessing, which he granted them, of course.

The last weekend at the church house was full of excitement. The *paroissien* brought more news of various celebrations taking place in Paris. Créteil was only thirteen kilometers from the "City of Light", and news traveled fast.

Pastor David gave a very touching *homélie* at Sunday's mass. He spoke about the human candor in serving God, delivering them from evil will. He also bestowed a special blessing on Suzanne and Émilie, to protect them on their trip to Paris.

When Tuesday morning finally broke in Créteil, Suzanne and Émilie were already at the train station together. Suzanne received a telegram from her fiancé that he would be in the parade on *avenue des Champs-Élysées*. She had not seen him for more than two months. He mentioned that he was to be relieved from France and sent back to the United States to be trained for the final defeat of the Axis forces. She was hoping that he would ask her to come with him and get married in Mississippi, where he was from. Robert Hopkins spoke French, like many people living in that region of the United States of America, and she was certain that she would fit in.

Soon it was time. The 6:50 a.m. train for Paris was in front of them. The station was crowded with French soldiers, Allied soldiers, men, women, and children. Everyone wanted to see the parade. The fare was free that day. It was a day of liberation. Suzanne and Émilie boarded the wagon at once. The atmosphere was purely festive. Wine and champagne flowed generously, even though it was early in the morning. They would arrive in Paris in thirty minutes.

༺*Émilie's Journal*༻

Dear Journal,

I came to Creteil to find Antoine. What I found was the third secret of love and happiness, the gift of communication!

The loss of Antoine's love was, for the most part, my fault. My communication style, which had been filled with the deadliest sins of all, judgment and criticism, gave him cause to not stay with me. His duty called first and very little held him to me. God came to my rescue and brought amazing new friends who embodied all the aspects of amitiée durable. *Perhaps I was the one that attracted them to me. I know that they came into my life for a reason: to help me on my journey to the French* art de l'amour. *Now that I have made a PACT with communication and grasped the gift of understanding, I feel that I can be in a healthy relationship with my loved one.*

I will never use the sins of communication again. I understand how their dark powers can destroy not only a message but also a relationship.

I have learned so much and yet know that so much more will need to be learned on my journey to the French art de l'amour. *I am grateful for my ability to stay open-minded and invite great things into my life. I am forever appreciative of how far I have come.*

My dear Journal, I am transposing the summary of my learning to you so that, one day, I may read you with a smile, maybe to someone in need.

Maman *often talked to me about being my own best friend and the power of being a friend to others. I found the embodiment of her definition in my new friend, Suzanne. In her, I found the golden principles of an* amitiée durable*:*

-Honest-
Where I know, no matter what, she'll tell me the truth, even if it's sometimes painful.

-Trustworthy-
Knowing that we will always be honest with each other.

-Loyal-
No matter what she will never betray me. I will forever be the same to her and never turn my back on her.

-Dependable-
Her words mean everything. I know I can depend on Suzanne. I can depend on her integrity.

-Empathetic-
I truly appreciate her ability to see the world from my viewpoint.

-Non-judgmental-
I never feel judged when I am with her. I can truly open myself up and reveal my innermost secrets. I have shared so many intimate memories with Suzanne, especially the ones about Antoine, and never felt I was being inappropriate. Not even once.

-Good listener-
Suzanne is an amazing communicator. Time and time again, she uses the PACT of communication with me. It feels amazing. It's a true gift.

-Supportive in good and bad times-
Above all else, I know she is there for me, even more so when I really need her. Her presence comforts me like a warm blanket on a cold winter night.

-Light in life-
We laugh and LAUGH about our little quirks. She is so much fun to be around. She always seizes the opportunity to bring lightness to life.

I also found a mentor in Captain (Pastor) John. He taught me about communication. I was lost and did not know it. He saw potential in me and in my ability to spread the gift of communication to others. His patience and wisdom made his teaching indélébile *(permanent).*

The PACT of communication that he offered me changed my life forever, and for that I will be eternally grateful. I know now that using healthy communication skills can make a difference in people's lives.

I am sitting on the train en route to Paris. I feel more ready than ever to find my true love, my soul mate. I've learned so much about relationships these past few months. All healthy relationships start with ME, first and foremost. I cannot attract love and happiness if I am not a safe haven for it. The power of self-love and being my own best friend are the foundation of any long lasting love.

Communication is an expression of the soul. PACT only helps with communicating your message. Empathy is the motivation. In intimacy, I have found another form of communication, my physical and spiritual desire to be as one with my love and also myself.

ಐ

The Fourth Secret Ring

Common Values and Goals *or* Looking at the World in the Same Direction

If there is one thing that is more important than anything else in a happy and loving relationship, it is the ability to share common goals and values. This critical element is the glue that will hold you together, keep you engaged in difficult situations, and celebrate your common accomplishments. Without it clearly defined, understood, and reaffirmed regularly, the relationship is doomed to stall and most likely collapse under the weight of its obligation. Your relationship will not be able to grow and mature. Even if you have mastered all the other elements (self-love, intimacy, and communication), a relationship without clear, shared, common goals and values will soon suffocate. Partners will soon ask, "Why are we together?" and "What are we trying to accomplish together?"

॰ഠ

Suzanne and Émilie enjoyed their fantastic journey to Paris. The atmosphere was one of celebration and liberation. Enjoying Paris' freedom was an aphrodisiac. They talked to everyone around them as if they knew them, sharing common stories and values of freedom.

They arrived just before 7:30 a.m. at the *Gare de Lyons*. Paris was in celebration. Music and laughter were everywhere. Émilie and Suzanne had never seen anything like it before.

They had a *rendezvous* at *rue Balzac* and *Champs-Élysée* at 1:00 p.m. This was the place where Robert arranged to meet Suzanne for the first time in a long while. She could not wait to see him again. Robert was in the armored division of the 8th U.S. Army. He had enrolled in late December, 1942 and had seen action ever since. He was to be on parade that afternoon right in front of them. Suzanne envisioned a magical moment.

Suzanne and Émilie went to a café near *rue Balzac*. It was charming. A man played accordion in front of the café and sang popular songs. The patrons sang along with him. A *joie-de-vivre* was very much present in Paris. Émilie craved the sort of fresh croissant and latte that could only be found in a Paris café. She went to the *garçon* and ordered two croissants and two *café au lait*, one for her and one for Suzanne, now her best friend. After a few minutes, Émilie brought the *petite gâterie* outside where they both sat. Suzanne was delighted. They saw people celebrating in the street all around them. Paris was euphoric. It was a liberation that the Parisians had been waiting for. It had taken more than four long years to come.

After few more *cafés au lait* and pastries, Suzanne and Émilie decided to go to their *rendezvous*.

Suzanne's heart was filled with anticipation to see Robert on his Sherman M4 tank. She had received many letters telling her about the fighting he endured to liberate France. He also talked about how much he loved her and how wonderful she was. He wrote, in intimate detail, of his longing for her alabaster skin and fiery red hair. Suzanne kept one special letter with her at all times. She knew all the words by heart. That particular letter was her port of hope in this sea of injustice and broken dreams. Robert expressed his deepest emotions toward her and asked her to be his wife. He made a pledge to marry her in Paris.

Rue Balzac and *Champs-Élysée* was only five minutes from the café. The streets were crowded. Everyone wanted to see their liberators. Suzanne and Émilie rushed to get to the exact location of the special *rendezvous*. It was only a question of time before Suzanne would be reunited with her fiancé. Émilie thought of Antoine and wondered where he was on this glorious day. Strangely, she did not feel much. Her memories were just a beautiful souvenir. Her heart had had a chance to heal, and she had matured. She had realized that healthy communication was a fundamental part of her journey to the French *art de l'amour*. Émilie was ready and excited to be surprised by life once more.

ಐ*French Secret*ಐ

Nobody is perfect! Knowing and growing is part of life.

It was close to 1:00 p.m. and the sky was of a perfect azure blue. There was not a cloud to be seen and the sun was at its zenith, in perfect harmony with the day ahead. Suzanne and Émilie watched the military police clear the avenue. Honoring the French for their suffering and their resistance to the enemy, the French Division under General de Gaulle led the parade in front of the entire 8th Army who would soon fill the avenue.

Suddenly a twenty-one-gun salute resonated near the *Arc de Triomphe*. The celebration had started. The Parisians started to sing the national anthem *la Marseillaise* as the French Division rolled down the Avenue. Paris had waited for this exact moment for a long time, and it had finally arrived. Émilie and Suzanne waved at the General passing by. Then, like a growling thunderstorm rolling in slowly, the U.S. Army approached. The spectacle was stunning. The Champs-Élysées was completely dwarfed by the immense military machine. Man after man, armor after armor, artillery pieces—and even seventy-seven slow flying P-51 Mustang fighter airplanes flew overhead. It was overwhelming.

The friends looked at each armored vehicle as it went by, hoping to see Robert's tank. Suzanne was wearing her beautiful red dress, the one she been wearing when Robert and she met for the first time. He would certainly recognize her amongst the millions of beautiful woman that were there. Then Suzanne recognized, from a distance, the white scarf that she had given Robert.

"Émilie! Look it's him. It's him! I think I see him! He's the tank commander with the white scarf," Suzanne repeated in excitement. Suzanne waved at him. He returned the gesture with both arms in the air. She was overjoyed and felt truly blessed. He was *chevaleresque*.

They continued to wave and blow kisses to each other. The Sherman tank slowly approached Suzanne and Émilie. It bore her name on the left side: *Little Suzie*. Suzanne started crying tears of joy. Robert was only about twenty yards from her. Unexpectedly, Robert climbed out of the turret, detached his earphones and jumped off the rolling tank. Suzanne and Émilie could not believe it. Her heart stopped momentarily. He ran to Suzanne. Robert did not say a word to her. He just grabbed her by the shoulders and gave her the most passionate kiss. The few seconds seemed eternal to Suzanne. She could not breathe.

Then Robert looked deep into her eyes and said, "Meet me here at 6:00 tonight for dinner."

Before Suzanne could reply he whispered in her ear in his American accent, "I love you my little Suzie. I love you so much!"

Suzanne was ready to faint. Robert turned and ran back to the rolling tank. He grabbed the access ladder, climbed into his turret and reconnected his earphones. Then he turned around and blew a few more kisses to her as they drove away.

Suzanne was speechless. She turned to Émilie and asked, "What just happened?" She was flustered by the event. Robert was a brave and romantic man, and Suzanne was madly in love with him.

ᛞ*French Secret*ᛞ

Passion is the essence of love. It's the essence of life. It's the petrol that fuels our souls.

Still in shock from Robert's actions, Suzanne and Émilie walked up to the *Arc de Triomphe*, seeking a closer view of the parade. Suzanne was pensive. She was replaying the most amazing moment of her life in her mind.

Émilie respected her time and did not interrupt her moment. She was truly happy for her. Suzanne was a great friend. She perfectly embodied the principles of the *amitiée durable*. Émilie also replayed the event in her mind, but from a different angle. She had noticed the tank commander behind Robert's vehicle. He was handsome. He was tall, with dark hair and blue eyes. They were a blue that she could drown herself in. He was also wearing a scarf, most likely a regimental one. He also had the funniest moustache, small but rolled up at each end. Most of all, he had a twinkle in his eye when he saw Émilie. That twinkle had started her mind racing. It was the first time since Antoine that a man had caught her attention. Émilie wanted to know more about him. Perhaps when Robert came back later that night she could ask him for more information.

Émilie and Suzanne stayed the whole afternoon *sur l'avenue Champs-Élysées*. The parade had finished, yet the Parisians continued to celebrate. It would be like this for the next few days. Afterward, it would be time to rebuild the lives that had been on hold. It would be time for people who had been separated to reunite. It would be time for dreams to finally come true.

Suzanne and Émilie's dreams were also about to come true in a large way.

At 6:00 p.m. Suzanne and Émilie waited exactly where they had seen Robert that afternoon. They sat at the café *Le Cochon Vert* (The Green Pig), waiting for Robert and Suzanne to be reunited. Émilie had other plans. She wanted to leave the two lovebirds without a chaperone. A night of walking the streets of the newly freed Paris sounded wonderful to her.

Robert showed up with a beautiful bouquet of roses just as they finished their espressos. He was still wearing his white scarf, but now wore his dress uniform. Suzanne jumped out of her seat and into his arms. This time, she took the lead. Their passionate kiss lasted for two minutes or more. Robert kissed her on her neck and ears. There was lots of giggling and plenty of love. Then, slowly stopping, Robert shyly whispered "Hi" to her. They held hands and looked into each other's eyes without blinking. They did not want to miss one more moment of seeing one another. Finally, they both stopped and sat at the table. Suzanne admired

The Four Secret Rings of Love and Happiness

and smelled her beautiful roses. Émilie was deeply touched. She wanted that type of love. She wanted fireworks and wings to lift her heart.

"Émilie, this is Captain Robert J. Hopkins of the 8th Army, Armor Corps division," Suzanne announced proudly.

"It's so nice to finally meet you. I've heard so much about you that I feel like I already know you," said Émilie graciously.

"It is very kind of you to say so, Émilie. Suzanne has a gift of surrounding herself with the greatest friends," Robert politely replied.

The discussion continued between the three of them for a little while. Robert asked the *garçon* to bring his best chilled champagne and three flutes. It was a time to reveal in happiness and savor the magical moment. When the waiter brought their *Veuve Cliquot 1927 Grand Crut*, they all clapped in celebration. Robert was given the honor of opening the bottle for the ladies. He served them first and then himself, like a gentleman.

Robert stood in the middle of the café and proclaimed, "I would like to propose a toast! To eternal love. May God, in his grace, reunite all true soul mates forever!"

Suzanne and Émilie both stood and raised their glasses. Robert took Suzanne in his arms and kissed her once more.

Émilie looked at Robert and Suzanne, and thought of the handsome tank commander.

"Robert, may I ask you who the officer was in the vehicle behind you with the funny moustache? Émilie asked bashfully.

Robert smiled back and said, "My good friend Captain Ryan Parker. He's from Chicago. We went to armor school together. He is a true and fine gentleman... and still available, I might add," Robert said with a wink. He continued, "We call him 'Bugle Boy'."

"Bugle Boy. That's a strange nickname," Émilie commented.

"Ryan was a music professor before the war, as was his father. Heck, I think his whole family plays music," Robert explained. "Ryan is the morale lifter of the division. Every morning at armor school, he would play first call and end it with a foxtrot rhythm. It would put a big smile on everyone's face, and the day always seemed to get better after that," Robert said nostalgically.

"He seems to be a fine man," Émilie agreed.

"Yes he is. Courageous like no other as well. He would take a bullet for his brothers in arms," Robert added, now turning his attention back to Suzanne, who had not stopped staring at him the entire time. "Now, where were we?" he asked his fiancée.

Émilie smiled, finished her champagne, and said, "I will leave you two lovebirds alone. The night is young and I want to embrace Paris. I will meet you here tomorrow at 9:00 a.m. Suzanne, if that is ok with you," Émilie asked.

"Yes, but be careful," Suzanne said, worrying for her.

Robert stood up and kissed Émilie's hand. "It was a pleasure meeting you. Thank you for being such a great friend to Suzanne while I was away," he said with genuine appreciation.

Émilie left the café and headed to see the Eiffel tower. She remembered the magnificent steel structure from when she was a child. It was a miracle that it had not been damaged during the war. She planned to walk along *la Seine* toward *la Cathédrale Notre-Dame*. *La Seine* was a nice place to relax and think. She needed some time for both. Now that Antoine was gone, she needed to think about her future after the war.

Émilie was only twenty-one and in her prime. Her whole life was in front of her. She wanted a family of her own. She also wanted a husband who would understand and appreciate her secrets. That was of the greatest importance to her. She knew who she was and that she possessed beautiful gifts to offer to a deserving prince charming.

All of this thinking made her hungry. She was close to the *Jardin des Tuileries* near *le Louvre*. Many restaurants were in full swing for the night. They each had their own individual charm, which made Paris such an incredible experience at night. The sun was setting, and the oil-lit street lamps began to flicker to life. The city was preparing for its second act.

Émilie's attention suddenly shifted to a beautiful little bistro close to *la Seine*. The exterior décor was sublime. *Le Pain d'Or* (The Golden Bread) was lit up over the door. The lettering was gold with a black background, and the entrance was a beautiful forest green with gold accents. It was truly charming. The interior was lit by candlelight. A magnificent aura surrounded the patrons. Everyone was smiling and having fun. She didn't have much money left and wanted to keep enough for the train back to St. Girons or perhaps Limoges, but she could not resist the invitation. Tonight was a very special night. Paris was celebrating and she couldn't miss it for anything.

She entered the *petit bistro* and was greeted with a smile by the *maître d'hôtel*.

"Good evening, Madame, a table for two?" asked the maitre d' politely.

"Just for one, thank you," replied Émilie.

"Very well. Please follow me," said the maître d'hôtel.

The bistro was filled to capacity but the gentleman found a table close to the fireplace where she could view the whole room. The interior was delightful. A golden aura filled it from floor to ceiling. The dimmed lighting of the candles made every conversation seem more pleasant and amiable. Everyone seemed happy and purposeful. It was like a dark veil had been lifted from the Parisians.

Émilie sat and thanked the gentleman. She looked around, absorbing the *joie de vivre*. The energy was euphoric. She looked at the menu on the table and decided to start with a glass of Cabernet Sauvignon paired with some cheddar cheese. The *garçon* came over when he saw Émilie had put down her menu. He graciously took her order and went to the kitchen. Émilie closed her eyes and absorbed the liberating energy. She was happy. She was happy even though she didn't know where she would be tomorrow. She was living in the moment.

When she opened her eyes, she noticed a very handsome man looking at her from across the room. He looked familiar. His eyes were kind and he had a smile that made her melt. Dressed in a tailored suit, he sat with two other U.S. military men. She wondered who he could be. He was not wearing a uniform. It was difficult to make out his face from such a distance, under candlelight. Émilie closed her eyes once more. The day had been eventful and she replayed the afternoon's parade in her mind.

Suddenly, she felt a presence near her. It was probably the *garçon* with her red wine. She opened her eyes and right in front of her stood the handsome man who was smiling at her. It was Ryan, the tank commander. Émilie was shocked. She closed her eyes again to make sure she wasn't dreaming. How could this be real? Paris had millions of people celebrating right now. Him being here was impossible. Then Ryan addressed her in a gentle tone.

"Bonsoir, Madame," he said with the most romantic voice she had ever heard. His French accent was perfect. Émilie opened her eyes slowly. He was there. He was really there! Her heartbeat accelerated. Her face flushed *écarlate*.

☙*French Secret*☙

The law of attraction is very real, especially in love. Intensely imagining the relationship you want will guide the energy towards its manifestation.

"I am sorry if I frightened you, Madame," Ryan said politely.

Émilie could not say a word as she looked into his deep blue eyes.

Ryan continued, "I am terribly sorry, but I think I saw you this afternoon at the parade. My good friend Robert was the one that jumped off the Sherman tank to kiss your friend."

Émilie had been struck by a thunderbolt, a *coup de foudre*. She did not know what to say or what to do. Here, in front of her, stood the most handsome man she had ever seen.

Émilie rallied to muster a few words. "You are not in uniform."

Ryan smiled and said, "I had clothes to change into at my grandmother's house. She lives close by. After the parade I went to change and say hi to Nanny."

Émilie was now more puzzled than ever. As she was about to ask another question, the *garçon* arrived with her wine and cheese.

Ryan apologized, "I am sorry to have disturbed you. I will go back and see my friends now".

Ryan turned and, as he was about to leave, Émilie pleaded loudly, "No, please. Don't go." She added, "I'm sorry. I am just so taken by your charm."

Ryan smiled and asked if he could join her. Émilie

welcomed him to her table. He asked her if he could order a bottle of champagne to celebrate the occasion. She joyfully agreed.

Émilie and Ryan talked and laughed without taking their eyes off each other. They spoke about everything. They discussed their pasts, where they grew up, their parents and friends. They also talked about what they had learned and what defined them. They discussed their values. They also spoke about what they wanted to do after the war ended. They explored their goals together.

Ryan wanted to go back and continue teaching music at Columbia University in Chicago. He also wanted to have a family like the one he grew up in. It was a place where happiness was always present. Ryan's dad had been a professor at the university for many years. In fact, he was now the dean.

Émilie also shared some of her secrets, although not all of them. She explained how self-love was important to her. She also shared her gift of communication that she had just received.

Ryan was educated and open-minded. He knew these concepts but he wanted to know more. He found Émilie extremely attractive, not only for her stunning looks but for her beautiful disposition and for her pure soul.

༺‎French Secret༻

Discussing your values and life goals early in the relationship is critical. It forms the initial foundation of a potential union. It is important from a compatibility perspective and also to assess whether the relationship is viable to pursue.

They talked and talked and talked some more. After the second bottle of champagne and a succulent dinner, the *garçon* told them that they were closing. It was 3:37 a.m.

The couple looked around and realized that they were the only ones left in the bistro. They hadn't noticed the patrons leaving. They were too enchanted with one another. A beautiful "love energy" had started to form around them. Ryan asked Émilie if she was too tired to continue talking. She was full of energy. Émilie asked Ryan if he wanted to walk with her the whole night and enjoy the most beautiful day of her life together. Ryan agreed whole heartily. It was, strangely, the most beautiful day of his life, as well.

After taking care of the bill, Ryan opened the door and intentionally took her hand, inviting her to explore their new romance. Émilie gasped. It was the first time since Antoine that a man had touched her. She missed it. She missed the secure feeling a fine gentleman can provide to a woman. Ryan was that gentleman. They both walked along the *la Seine* toward *Cathédrale Notre Dame*. The scenery was magical. Almost no one was on the street. It seemed as if Paris belonged to them and was guiding them on their new journey with its beautiful illumination.

Émilie and Ryan were now on the *Pont au Double* near the *Cathédrale Notre Dame*. It was by far her favorite site. The bridge linked Paris to the small island *l'Ile Notre Dame*. The little bridge had a unique charm and the scenery was breathtaking. Émilie stopped to look at the water passing under the bridge. Still holding her hand, Ryan turned Émilie to face him. The gentle light of morning shone in each other's eyes. Slowly, Ryan approached her lips. Émilie closed her eyes to feel the passion going through her. She invited him. A long and sensual kiss was the coronation of a perfect day, the most amazing day of their lives.

They were falling for each other, without boundaries. She had been waiting for this moment. She had been waiting for her true prince charming. They held hands and walked to the *cathédrale*, still talking and laughing about the day, about everything. Then, right in front of the entrance of Notre Dame, Ryan got down on one knee, holding Émilie's hand and looked into her big blue eyes.

"I promise you that one day I will marry you in this very church, where angels will resonate their trumpets of love and God will bless our divine union," Ryan vowed with clear conviction in his voice.

Strangely, Émilie was not surprised. It was as if she had been waiting for his announcement. Émilie smiled the purest smile and said, "I know you will," confidently.

Ryan stood up and embraced her passionately, once more.

As morning broke, the sunrise passed over the Eiffel Tower, beaming in splendor and blessing a glorious new day. It was 7:17 a.m. and they were starving. Ryan took Émilie for a *petit déjeuner* (breakfast). Many restaurants were just opening their doors and patrons were waiting to go in. This was the first day of their liberation. Many U.S. G.I.s were in Paris. Most of them had some time off in the City of Lights. Ryan and Robert had three weeks to get to know their adoptive city. After that, they were scheduled to go back to the U.S., Fort Benning, Kentucky for additional training. The invasion of Europe was one thing; the invasion of Japan would be a completely different story.

Émilie and Ryan were near the *rue Balzac* in a beautiful restaurant, *L'Oie Grasse* (The Fat Goose). They made plans to visit Ryan's *grand-maman* after seeing Suzanne at 9:00 a.m. The morning was perfect. In fact, everything was perfect when she was with Ryan. He was caring in his actions and in his ability to listen. Ryan also had the gift of communication.

After few croissants with *foie gras* and hot coffee, they went to their *rendezvous*. As they approached *rue Balzac*, they spotted Suzanne waiting on a park bench facing *avenue Champs-Élysées*. Émilie snuck up and covered her eyes, surprising her. Suzanne jumped up and laughed when she saw Émilie standing there. After the usual kisses, Émilie introduced Ryan to Suzanne. They spent some time telling the story that led to their encounter. Suzanne was taken by the incredible coincidence. Émilie, her best friend, was to stay in her life for much longer than they thought.

The couples spent considerable time together over the course of the next several days. Ryan and Robert were on leave in Paris and they had the loves of their lives with them. Life could not get any better.

After meeting Suzanne, Ryan took Émilie to see his favorite Nana. She lived near the *Quartier Latin*. Her apartment was charming. Lilly, short for Lilianne, lived alone. Her husband had died in the Great War near Belgium. She never remarried, but rather dedicated the rest of her life to the memories of her husband. Lilly was a well-known artist in Paris. She loved the Impressionist school of painting. Her favorite painting was the *Water Lilies* by Monet.

When Ryan and Émilie arrived at the apartment, Lilly was overwhelmed to see them. After a formal introduction and an espresso, Lilly took Émilie and showed her painting collection. Ryan took the opportunity to get fresh clothing for the day.

Lilly took to Émilie immediately. Her gentle nature and kind spirit connected with Nana instantly. Lilly invited Émilie and Ryan to stay for lunch. She had made his favorite, *soup aux onions gratinée* (French onion soup). Ryan was excited. Grandma's soup was to die for. Her secret ingredients were generous portions of cognac and red wine, stewing the caramelized onions for hours. Ryan always had seconds.

After lunch, Ryan asked Nana if they could both stay with her while he reported to the *École Militaire*. Émilie was exhausted. All of the emotions from a long night in Paris with Ryan had taken the best out of her. She would have the most wonderful dreams. She felt safe and protected.

While at the *École Militaire* in Paris, Ryan and Robert went over preparations for their return to the US. Their training for the Pacific campaign was scheduled for three months. During that time, they would practice improved maneuvers that had been specially adapted for that type of warfare. Ryan and Robert were excited to go back home, and this time they were bringing a special gift from their European campaign.

Émilie was at Lilly's, helping her with supper. She really liked Ryan's grandma. Lilly reminded her of her mother, Michelle, in many ways. Lilly practiced the art of self-love on a daily basis. She was always positive, and her love for her lost husband was *immuable* (enduring). He had died nearly thirty years earlier, and her devotion to him was the same as the day she married him. It fascinated Émilie. Her parents had a strong relationship as well. They had arguments, of course, but always came back together with a smile and never resented each other. However, Lilly's devotion to the love of her life was on a completely different scale. She had grieved for him many years before but his spirit and love still lived within her. Émilie wanted to know more about her relationship. She wanted to get some advice about how to create a marriage that was durable beyond death.

ᛰFrench Secretᛰ

True love transcends time. True love is the embodiment of the Four Secret Rings in human form.

Émilie and Lilly prepared a roast. That evening's dinner would be dedicated to family and love. As they completed preparing supper, Émilie seized the opportunity to ask Lilly about her husband and how she kept her love so pure.

"Nanny Lilly, tell me about your husband and how he was with you," Émilie asked.

Lilly sighed and smiled. "Arthur was an exceptional man. He was a man of many virtues. We were married the first week we met. I fell completely in love with his spirit and his *chevaleresque* ways." She continued to reminisce. "What was exceptional about him was his ability to talk and listen responsively. We spent so much time talking about our dreams and how to build them together. The connection was instant. We always stayed true to the purpose of our union and spent time maintaining our love".

ஐ*French Secret*ஐ

In order to keep your relationship solid and grounded to your purpose, you must keep the objective of your union in mind. Without common values and goals, the relationship will likely stall and eventually fall apart.

Émilie was extremely curious and wanted to know more.

Nanny Lilly added, seeing Émilie so inquisitive, "You see, Émilie, love and marriage is easy if you marry your best friend. When both people exude the characteristics of a true friend and share common goals and values, love and happiness will find its way to them. And let's not forget amazing daily intimacy!"

Émilie and Lilly started to laugh out loud. They really had fun together.

Émilie was beginning to understand and appreciate what it took to have a loving and happy relationship. The last secret was the culmination of self-love, intimacy, and communication. When they came together, it resulted in finding and holding common goals and values.

ஐ*French Secret*ஐ

The secret recipe for a long and happy marriage is quite simple:

5 parts *healthy self-love*
1 part *intimacy*
2 parts *strong communication skills*
1 part *common goals and values*

Mix these ingredients together and you get:

<u>Eternal Love and Happiness,</u> voilà*!*

It was close to dinnertime, and Émilie couldn't wait to see Ryan again. All the talk of love and relationships made her feel blessed to have found him. As her thoughts turned to Ryan, he appeared through the door with two bouquets of roses, one for Émilie and the other for Nanny Lilly. As they took their flowers, they both gave him a kiss on both cheeks.

"You are so wonderful and thoughtful, Ryan," Nanny Lilly said.

Émilie took Ryan's head in both hands and gave him a passionate kiss.

Lilly was happy for them. She remembered the days when Arthur came home with flowers. It made her feel special and wanted. Émilie felt the same way.

Classical music filled the little apartment, as did joy and laughter. Émilie prepared the table while Lilly put the last touches on the succulent dinner. Then they heard a pop from across the room. Ryan had brought a bottle of *Veuve Clicquot* champagne. He took three glasses with gold rims and slowly poured the happy nectar.

Ryan cleared his throat for a toast, "I would like to propose a toast to our family. May God bless my love, Émilie. She is a precious treasure that I found in Paris. We are like two vessels in the dark of night guided only by the light of love. My promise to you, once more, Émilie, is to marry you before we leave Paris," Ryan said, holding his glass high. Émilie simply nodded in confirmation of his pledge. Then, to seal his word, Ryan grabbed Émilie by the waist and kissed her like she had never been kissed before.

The evening was one of celebration. Ryan was particularly funny. He acted out skits that brought everyone to laughter. Lilly shared interesting stories about her past as a young girl growing up in Paris in the *Belle Époque*. She also shared some stories about when Ryan was a young boy. Émilie grew fonder of him by the hour. Lilly also mentioned that she would need to take the train to Nice the next evening to help her daughter with her grandchildren. She invited them to stay for the duration of Ryan's vacation in Paris. Ryan, like a gentleman, asked for Émilie's consent to stay with him. Émilie did not decline. However, she did not agree right away either. Ryan had to prove his worthiness, protection, and love for her before she was to reveal her intimate secret.

As the hour grew late, Émilie and Ryan made plans for the next day. Lilly was also tired. She could not remember the last time she laughed so much. She retired to her bedroom after giving each of them a kiss goodnight.

The next day, Émilie woke up early. Ryan had given the guest room to her and slept on the sofa. Respect for Émilie's space was a priority. It was a matter of emotional intimacy.

She went to Ryan and, to wake him up, gave him a gentle kiss on the lips.

Ryan smiled.

"Good morning my love," said Émilie, smiling back.

"Good morning, angel," he replied.

"How do you like your breakfast?" Émilie asked.

"The way you like it," Ryan responded. Their harmony was perfect. Ryan held her while she cooked breakfast. They were inseparable. They were in love.

The day was exhilarating. Paris was a happy place to be. Holding hands, they spent time visiting everything Paris had to offer. More importantly, they spent time talking about their future. Ryan was scheduled to go back to the U.S. in seventeen days, and Émilie wanted to know if he was going to be the one to take her away. She wasn't about to wait, this time. She had matured and was ready for her new life, but only with her true love. Ryan had made his intentions clear. Émilie needed to be ready to accept him without doubt.

Ryan was a great communicator. He always took the time to listen to Émilie and ensure he understood her feelings, desires, and needs. He was also great at making plans and clarifying each other's values. It was important for him to ensure she was happy in their new relationship. Émilie was learning the last secret of love and happiness from Ryan. Reviewing common goals and values was something that had not been done with Antoine. They knew that the future was uncertain for them. Why create hope when no one had control over the immediate future?

This time it was different. Opportunity had presented itself to them.

❧*French Secret*❧

The gift of communication is the key that opens the door to the last secret, common goals and values. Please, never forget this!

Émilie had brought her journal and was making notes about all of their discussions and insights. She liked journaling. She liked capturing and reflecting the progress of their conversations. She found it interesting and revealing.

They arrived at the Louvre museum for a visit. Ryan had heard about it and always wanted to experience it. Émilie had visited this magnificent place of culture when she was young. However, she had not been as interested as she was now. Ryan was an art connoisseur. He was well educated and fascinated by the artists of the past. Émilie and Ryan gradually improved their vision of the future.

Émilie felt, more and more, that she belonged with Ryan.

The picture was becoming clearer as they discussed their likes and dislikes. Émilie knew that within two weeks she would be asked to depart to another world, the United States of America. It was a euphoric feeling. She was starting to think that teaching French to Americans would be wonderful. Sharing her gift with others was a perfect profession for her.

ҽ⃝French Secretҽ⃝

Here is Ryan's secret for aligning common goals and values. The most important element when aligning goals and values is, first, to know them. What defines you? What do you want to accomplish as a person in the next year? What is your vision in terms of accomplishments in a new relationship? Second, clearly itemize all of your values and goals. This can be done with the help of your journal and is extremely important before you meet that special someone. It will not only help clarify your objectives with this person but also give you clues to the viability of the potential relationship.

Everything starts with you, just like the secret of self-love.

Ryan and Émilie had a wonderful time together that day. They talked and laughed and enjoyed each other's company. They spoke in detail about their memories and their vision of a future together. They took the time to get to know each other's wants and dreams. Émilie was falling in love with Ryan. He was exactly what she wanted her man to embody, her very best friend. She was ready to deliver to Ryan one of her secrets.

Later that day, they arrived back at the apartment. Ryan went to the gramophone and put on a jazz record. The mood of the apartment changed to romance as soon as the sweet music began to play.

Émilie approached Ryan from behind, kissing his neck gently. He turned around and embraced her. Holding each other tight, they swayed to the rhythm. When the record finished Ryan retrieved the bottle of Cabernet they bought that day. He poured Émilie's glass first, then his. Gazing into each other's eyes, they kissed once more. After taking a small sip of wine, Émilie took Ryan's glass in her hand and went toward the bedroom.

"Come with me, my love. I will show one of my secrets," Émilie said seductively.

Ryan followed and closed the door behind them. He lit some candles in the room to intensify the mood.

Émilie stood in front of Ryan and started to undress him and slowly kiss his body as she revealed each part. When she was done, Ryan did the same to her. Émilie was leading Ryan to her secret. Physical intimacy was one of the gifts she was ready to share with her worthy future husband.

The week flew by quickly. Émilie and Ryan had become soul-tied. They explored all the principles of a healthy relationship together. Between visiting friends, sharing meals at various bistros, communicating, and solidifying their union, they seemed to have no secrets left to be uncovered.

Sunday, September 10th was a magnificent day. The sun was warm and bright. Émilie and Ryan woke up in each other's arms, to the sound of the birds chirping. They made passionate love, like every morning, before eating their breakfast together. Émilie loved taking care of Ryan, and he reflected it back to her, hundred fold.

That morning, he invited Émilie to go to mass at Saint-Germain-des-Prés, the oldest church in Paris. It dated back to 542 AD. Ryan had something special in his pocket. After strolling the neighborhood for few hours, they stopped in the middle of a beautiful bridge called *Pont des Arts*. Ryan took Émilie's hand, reached into his pocket and took out Nanny Lilly's wedding ring. She had given it to him before she left.

Ryan knelt and said, "These past weeks have been a dream and *présage* of our future to come. I love you and will protect you with all my being. Will you marry me?"

Émilie, crying tears of joy, answered, "It would be an honor to be your wife for the rest of eternity. I trust your love and devotion to me as I will devote my entire being to you and our relationship."

He took Émilie's left hand and slipped the beautiful emerald and diamond engagement ring onto her finger. She continued to cry. She could not believe it was actually happening. So much joy and love was blessed upon them.

༺*French Secret*༻

True love exists. You must be ready to receive it!

The rest of the day was magical. They spent their time simply enjoying each other's company. After their full day together, they took a break on *Champ-de-Mars*, a beautiful park facing the Eiffel Tower. As they looked at the structure, they spoke about the beauty that was in front of them. The monument resonated with Ryan. A conversation that he had with Émilie earlier triggered a metaphor in his mind.

"I see this beautiful piece of art that has passed the test of time, like the purpose of our union," Ryan reflected.

Émilie was puzzled. "Tell me more, Ryan. It's intriguing."

Ryan continued, "Our love is the same as this immense tower in front of us. The four pillars represent the four foundations of love and happiness in a relationship, self-love, intimacy, communication, and common goals and values. All four pillars reach upwards and become one at its summit, the true expression of love and happiness."

Émilie agreed with Ryan's observation and liked the idea of the renowned Eiffel Tower standing as representation of their love.

Ryan and Émilie had a little more than a week before they left for America. Émilie sent a telegram to her *maman* and aunt, telling them the great news. She also informed them of the marriage that would take place on Tuesday, September 19th at the *Cathédrale Notre-Dame*. It was to be a special wedding ceremony. Suzanne and Robert were to be married at the same time. The following day, the men were scheduled to depart for America. They would leave from the port of Cherbourg, and Suzanne and Émilie would take the RMS Queen Elizabeth to New York, two days later.

The rest of week was extremely busy for Émilie and Ryan. There was so much to do before the grand departure into their new life. Between the preparations for the wedding ceremony and the immigration paperwork to be filled out, they both had a full workload. However, they still made it a priority to come together every day and give each other the gift of love-making.

Every day, Émilie wrote down all of the fantastic events she was experiencing in her journal and noted the wonderful teachings that life was unveiling to her. Soon enough, it was that special day. Émilie and her family were to meet at the *cathédrale,* where her father would walk her down the aisle. Émilie and Suzanne both dressed in white. Michelle had found her wedding dress and brought it with her from St. Girons.

༄French Secret༄

Journaling has so many therapeutic advantages. It is an integral part of your journey to The Four Secret Rings of Love and Happiness.

The men wore their brand new uniforms and waited at the altar for their soon-to-be wives. The *cathédrale* doors opened as the famous *Arrival of the Queen of Sheba* by Händel began to resonate throughout the church. Everyone stood as Émilie and Suzanne came into the light like two angels from heaven.

The ceremony was very emotional. Michelle and Renée had not seen their daughter for some time, and she was about to be married and leave for America. Michelle did not give away tears of sadness, but ones of joy. She always knew her daughter would find her way to love and happiness with her true soul mate.

As the priest pronounced the vows, Émilie remembered her journey from St. Girons to here. She was happy, but most of all proud of her commitment to herself of keeping an open mind. She had a new sense of security. Ryan looked into her beautiful blue eyes and gently slid a gold band around her finger. The ring represented the coronation of her journey. Her wedding ring symbolized her common goals and values with Ryan, her fourth and final secret ring to love and happiness.

҂*Émilie's Journal*҂

Dear Journal,

I am leaving for America tomorrow, as a wife. I came to Paris to celebrate victory over evil. Sometimes I think the evil was mine and my journey to Paris led me to conquer it. Now I am celebrating life.

I took a chance, a risk, by letting destiny lead me. After I left Créteil with Suzanne, I knew that something amazing was about to happen in my life. The more I learned about the French art de l'amour *principles, the more I became confident in my search for love. It's not that I was looking for it desperately.*

Love found me naturally, when I was ready.

Every day, I embraced self-love. I rejoiced being intimate with myself, but also with my love being one emotionally, spiritually and physically. I also give the gift of communication to others. Now that I have found the fourth and final secret to love and happiness, my relationship with Ryan is immuable.

My dear husband, my very best friend, was right. The Eiffel Tower is the perfect monument to represent the principles of the French art de l'amour *working together in unison.*

The last principle of the French art de l'amour is fundamental to the success and longévité of any relationship. It is a bridge between two souls coming together to create love. The strength of that bridge is directly proportionate to the commonality of our goals and values.

Ryan and I have spent a lot of time discussing our values and clarifying what defines us as people. Knowing myself, which largely stems from self-love, helped me share these values with him. I applied my gift of communication to understand his values and vision for our relationship. We have a PACT with communication. It was only through our PACT that we realized we had common values. Through our conversations, we learned that we embody the values of an amitiée durable: *honesty, trustworthiness, empathy, good listening, and so on.*

We also talked about our goals. I paid close attention to how important these were to Ryan. His showing of integrity and character gave me confidence that I could trust the pursuit of our common goals. I know that Ryan did the same for mine. Relationship goals are the glue that keeps people together in good and bad times.

<u>*Selfishness has no place in any healthy relationship.*</u>

Our first goal was to get married before leaving Paris, which we did. Our second goal was for me to move to the United States of America, which I am doing tomorrow. We have many other goals that will propel us to bigger ones as a couple, as husband and wife.

During our conversations, Ryan and I always came back to our need to share our knowledge and teach others. Ryan was already a professor, and I wanted to share the beautiful French language with America. We want to give our knowledge to others.

Teaching the French art de l'amour and our secrets to our children are also crucial.

I am excited to think that my child will not need to experience all the unnecessary mistakes that I have made. This thought warms my heart. Self-love will be their first step on this magnificent journey. Ryan and I agreed to provide them with fertile ground to grow strong and healthy.

Lately, I have been thinking about the word marriage *and its power. It is a very interesting word that holds a great deal of symbolism and truth. I have discovered that the word originated from the old French* marier *or the act of coupling two separate entities to make a new one... a better one, a stronger one. It makes me smile when I think of this undeniable truth about coming together in a relationship. The sum of all the parts working together always exceeds the value of the individual components. Common goals and values are the* marier *factor. The stronger and more common the goals, the stronger the relationship will become, standing the test of time.*

My dear Journal, I am leaving in the morning to another world, trusting God and his good faith.

Ryan is my rock and, with him, I'm ready to continue my journey in the French art de l'amour.

☙

Gabrielle's Journey

The greatest gift of all is the ability to give back to others, to make a difference in someone's life. The French art de l'amour *gives you this opportunity.*

Émilie dreamt of guiding her daughter along this journey. Her own mother, Michelle, did wonders to lay the foundation. It was now time for Émilie and Ryan to prove the power of these four secrets. These covenants go beyond creating love and happiness in your relationship; they are set to bring love and happiness to the people surrounding you. You become a role model for everyone in your life.

ஓ

March 07, 1961. Chicago was a very busy city at the time. So much had happened since the war ended. Émilie and Ryan were more in love with each other than ever. They made a point of practicing the French *art de l'amour* daily. Their marriage was one of trust, friendship, and happiness.

Émilie had taken a position as a French teacher at the University of Columbia, where Ryan was a music professor. The journey from France to the United States had gone well. After their arrival in New York, they went to Fort Benning, Kentucky for the remainder of the war.

Émilie had always wanted to teach French, and she found her first job as a translator at the headquarters. A few months later, she became a French substitute teacher for the officers going to France.

Ryan went on to be a Division Armor Commander. His exemplary character won him many honors and medals. He rose to the rank of colonel and was soon enough in charge of the Fort Benning Armored Division in Kentucky.

Ryan was an excellent communicator and motivator. The word *impossible* did not exist in his vocabulary. Neither did *retreat*. "ALWAYS move forward" was his motto for the troops. Ryan was also an avid reader. He dedicated one hour per day to self-growth or self-improvement. His favorite book was *Think and Grow Rich* by Napoleon Hill. In fact, he liked it so much that every new officer was given a copy when they came to Fort Benning.

☏French Secret☏

"Think and Grow Rich" by Napoleon Hill is a book to read and re-read. It has passed the test of time and its impact on humanity is well beyond measure.

Ryan and Émilie received a beautiful surprise eight months after their arrival at the base. Émilie gave birth to a lovely and healthy baby girl, weighing 8 pounds, 7 ounces. They named her Gabrielle. The meaning of her name resonated with Émilie. It was her little angel that she had been waiting so long for. Émilie always wanted to be a mother. She had an incredible role model in her own mother, Michelle.

She dreamt about taking time to teach her children the valuable lessons of life. Like her mother, she shared her gift responsibly, emphatically, and proactively with Gabrielle. Giving and teaching others was her calling in life.

Gabrielle grew up in Chicago, near Columbia University. Since her grandfather, father, and mother were all working at the university, it made sense to be close to this sanctuary of knowledge. Growing up, Gabrielle's favorite place was the University library. Émilie brought her there each day, and Madame Poirier looked after her. In between assisting the library personnel, Madame Poirier taught French to Gabrielle and the other children. Madame Poirier also came from France. She had moved to the United States soon after the invasion of Normandy. She had seen too many lives lost and too much destruction to bear. She wanted a fresh start with her husband, who took a position as a mathematics professor.

Émilie and Ryan were excellent educators and excelled in their fields of expertise. What was more, they both proved to be knowledgeable leaders who inspired the people around them. These were acquired skills that became the purpose in their lives. This purpose became an invaluable benchmark for their daughter. Gabrielle was a bit rebellious and sometimes headstrong. Telling her what to do or trying to control her would have pushed her the other way. However, they knew how to inspire her. They understood her gifts. The ability to lead Gabrielle's personality made the journey to the French *art de l'amour* even more fulfilling.

Émilie and Ryan raised their little angel to understand healthy self-love from a very young age. Every day brought its own joy, and Gabrielle displayed her transformation through action. Mother and daughter also had a ritual at teatime. Émilie would take her journal and read some of her daily entries. Gabrielle was particularly fond of the time when her mom and dad met in Paris. The famous "Paris by night" was her favorite story. It made her wonder how she would meet her own future soul mate.

৪০*French Secret*৪০

Self-love is foundation of all personal growth.

One of the first lessons that Émilie wanted to translate for Gabrielle was the gift to be her own best friend. As Michelle often said to Émilie, "You can't be a true friend to others if you are not a true friend to yourself."

This life lesson never left Gabrielle. The gift of being your own best friend is powerful. Using the principle of *amitiée durable* to guide and enrich your journey within is an important foundation of the French *art de l'amour*. Loving and caring for oneself is the essence of loving others in the purest way.

As Gabrielle started to use and embody the principles of *amitiée durable* and became her own best friend, many interesting things began to happen in her life.

First, she noticed that many of her so-called friends left her side. They could not hold up to her expectations of *amitiée durable*. She quickly recognized friendship that was worthy in others, and the value of true friendship. New friends began to gravitate to her. Not surprisingly, most of them had a special gift to share with her, as well. They were also from good families with sound values. Like attracted like.

In early May, 1961, Gabrielle's birthday was fast approaching. She was maturing and her personality was an expression of her inner growth. She was blooming like a beautiful cherry tree in spring. Émilie was not sure what gift she would get for her daughter. Strangely, Gabrielle did not want any gifts. She knew that she was loved and cherished. She did not need gifts to remind her of her beautiful blessings.

One morning, before class, Émilie stopped at a bookstore near the university. She loved to read and always searched for the next novel to bring home and share with the family. This particular bookstore was special to her. It was where she had worked when she arrived in Chicago after the war. She knew and was friends with all the staff, and addressed them by their first names. That morning Beatrice, her long-time acquaintance from purchasing, asked Émilie to follow her. After the usual catching up, she mentioned that they had received a very special shipment from France. Émilie was dying to learn more.

"You remember our supplier from St. Girons, Monsieur Vaillant?" Beatrice asked in her southern accent, noticeably unable to hold her excitement. "Come and see what he sent."

They both approached the mysterious package beside the wall at the back of the store. It was well-traveled and covered with all the stamps for America.

"You know what the strangest thing about it is?" Beatrice noted. "It's dated 1946. What's more, it has a note for you inside."

Émilie couldn't believe it. How could it be possible? It must have been sent the first year Émilie worked at the bookstore. She had kept in correspondence with Mr. Vaillant back in France, but…

"Read the letter! Read the letter in the box," insisted Beatrice.

September 25, 1946

Dear Émilie,

I am happy to see that you are settling well in your new country. St. Girons is not the same without you. I remember when you used to come over to the store and ask me for the latest books.

You always wanted to read the "grand authors", as you used to call them. One day, your mother asked me if I had a very special journal for you. I still remember that day. It was a gift that she wanted to give you before you left for Limoges. She wasn't sure if she would ever see you again. Her intent was that the journal would be your record through time.

We just received a box full of these journals and I thought you would appreciate giving them to your friends or selling them.

P.S. Let me know if they are the same. I am pretty sure they are.

Maurice

Émilie began to cry in disbelief. She was overwhelmed with joy. Beatrice tried to comfort her and felt bad that she had brought these emotions upon her. Émilie felt like the mysterious box had a purpose, an inspiration to the French *art de l'amour*. As Émilie settled down, Beatrice took out one of the beautiful red journals with gold lettering, put the letter inside, and gave it to Émilie. It had the exact same look and feel as the one she had received twenty years before. She thanked Beatrice for both the special moment and the gift.

Beatrice had an idea. "Émilie, with your permission, I would like to place these journals in our bookstore. I would like to call them the 'Émilie's Journal,'" said Beatrice, hoping for a positive answer.

Émilie agreed but suggested a more appropriate name. "Please call them 'The French *Art de l'Amour* Journal: a Calling to your Destiny' as a testament to my journey," Émilie replied, smiling.

"We will tell the story to our customers. I'm sure they will appreciate it," Beatrice added.

Émilie walked home, holding the precious journal, thinking about her episode at the bookstore. She was mentally exhausted, yet pensive. So many beautiful memories rushed through her mind. She felt blessed by all the lessons she had been able to capture in her beloved journal. Then, like a thunderbolt, an idea came to her.

"That's it! That's it!" she exclaimed in her charming French accent. "Gabrielle! This is a gift sent to her," Émilie shrieked as she quickened her step.

She arrived home out of breath and rushed to Ryan to share the magical moment with him. He could not believe the incredible timing and good fortune. He found the note to be inspiring.

As Émilie shared her intent to give Gabrielle the journal for her birthday, Ryan came up with an idea of his own.

"A beautiful fountain pen," he proposed. "Like the one your father gave you."

Émilie was overjoyed. It was a brilliant idea. As always, Ryan and Émilie were connected to one another mentally and spiritually. So much had happened since they met in Paris. The French *art de l'amour* kept them happy and in love with each other, and Gabrielle was the fruit of their eternal bond.

A day passed, and it was their daughter's birthday. Émilie knew Gabrielle's teacher very well and asked her if she could throw a surprise party for the occasion. Miss Blanchard agreed joyfully. Gabrielle was, like her name, an angel. She had many good friends and was truly loved and cherished by all of them.

The celebration at school was fun for all of the kids and parents, and Gabrielle received many gifts from her friends. She was gracious and appreciative of each of the offerings. As the celebration came to an end, Émilie whispered a secret into Gabrielle's ear, which made her smile. Her mother had an extra gift for her at home.

Gabrielle and Émilie held hands as they walked home from school. They had a French song they used to sing. It always made them laugh. When they got home, Gabrielle went to do her homework while Émilie prepared supper for the family. That night, she served Gabrielle's favorite meal: French cabbage rolls the way Nanny Michelle used to make them.

Suddenly the door opened and Ryan entered the kitchen.

"*Bonjour, mon amour*," he said, taking Émilie by the waist and giving her a passionate kiss. It had been their ritual ever since they met seventeen years before.

As they sat for supper, Émilie turned off all the lights. Gabrielle came downstairs with the feeling that something magical was about to happen. Both Émilie and Ryan started to sing "*Bonne Fête*". Gabrielle couldn't hold back her smiles at the sight of her parents singing for her and holding each other close. Her birthday cake, made by Émilie, was pink and white with strawberries. Gabrielle found it strange that there was only one candle on the cake rather than sixteen. As they finished the song, she asked why there was only one candle.

"You are the one and only," Ryan and Émilie said in unison.

Gabrielle smiled and blew out the candle.

A box wrapped in gold paper was lying on the table. It was fairly large and well decorated.

"Is that for me?" Gabrielle asked.

"Of course it's for you, my angel." Ryan and Émilie reached out and presented the box to her.

"This is very special, Gabrielle. It came all the way from France," Émilie said.

Gabrielle was extremely excited now. She took the box and carefully unwrapped it.

Gabrielle's eyes began to well at the sight of the gift. She recognized the texture and the bright red color of the object under the wrapping paper. A note was attached to the journal. Ryan and Émilie did not say a word. They let the moment sink in. Gabrielle started to read the letter aloud. She was not sure how to interpret it. Who was Maurice? The letter was dated 1946, a year after she was born. Gabrielle couldn't stand the mystery any longer.

"*Maman*, what does this mean?"
Émilie happily answered,

"Destiny!"

Gabrielle reached over, grabbed her parents, and kissed them. "You are the best parents that anyone could ever wish for."

"There's another gift for you. Look carefully," Ryan said with a smile.

Gabrielle looked under the wrapping paper. She noticed another gift, wrapped in purple and gold, with a bow attached. She opened her precious gift.

"A Mont-Blanc Meisterstrück!" she gasped. On the side of the fountain pen she noticed some engraving. It simply read

"Clarity".

Gabrielle asked what the meaning of the inscription was.

"You will see," answered Ryan.

The journal looked new but the smell of the paper gave away its age. She opened the cover and admired the beautiful cream and gold craft paper. An inscription was on the first page, written in cursive:

"Purity".

She turned to her mother, recognizing her handwriting, "*Maman*, what do you mean?"

Émilie replied, "You will see."

Gabrielle smiled and began to leaf through the pages.

❧*French Secret*❧

Clarity and purity are the gift of journaling daily.

The second page held the inscription,

"Self-Love is my first step in the French Art de l'amour... tell more..."

Gabrielle understood the meaning of this note. Émilie and her mother had been discussing the meaning and practice of self-love for years. She remembered seeing her mother touch her silver ring every morning. Her ritual was no secret to Gabrielle. She knew what her mother was doing. It was her special moment to focus on the five principles of self-love.

Gabrielle had had a journal all her life. She loved taking time to reflect on what happened to her each day. As her dad would say to her, "The grand masters of this world always write in their journals. It helps them keep perspective on current events and learn about themselves. If it's good for them, it will be good for you, Gabrielle."

However, this new journal was different. This was a journal that traveled through time to find her, to guide her, and to support her on her journey. Her mother was her spiritual leader and, through this special journal, her voice and guidance was present and would lead her along the path to the French *art de l'amour*.

Gabrielle felt loved by everyone around her. She was at peace with the woman she was becoming. She wanted to share her innermost thoughts about how she lived self-love daily. She opened her new journal and started to write after "tell me more...".

Every morning, I remind myself that I am response-ABLE. I have the ability to choose how I respond to what is happening in my life, which gives me greatest sense of power. I never feel like a victim. I always assume responsibility for everything that happens in my life, directly or indirectly, with no exceptions and no excuses. I create and attract the present moment. Therefore, I also have the power to change it if I am not pleased with the outcome.

She continued to write, *I love taking a few minutes to review at least five things that I am appreciative of and blessed by. My mother and father are always at the top of the list. After all, they have led me to be the person I am today and serve as inspiration for who I want to become. I am also appreciative of being my own best friend and exult the personality traits of my best friend.*

Loyalty and integrity to myself are also on the top of my list. I try to always do what I say and say what I do. This way my friends and family can count on me and trust me.

Gabriele put her journal down for few minutes. She wanted take some time to reflect on self-forgiveness and on her ability to self-improve. These two principles of self-love were extremely important to her. Gabrielle was known to never hold grudges or bad feelings towards others or herself. These feelings are a common trait of a victim mentality. She felt that the more you focus on such feelings, the more you attract the same. Forgiving yourself and others is crucial. It was her way to let go and be at peace.

Self-improvement was one of her favorite principles. Lately, Gabrielle had been focusing on her communication and presentation skills. She gave many speeches as the president of the Leadership Youth of Chicago. She had been reading books about how to give a spectacular and engaging speech, and logged many entries in her journal with tips and tricks to keep her audience attentive.

Gabrielle was very proud of who she was becoming. Self-appreciation, or the ability to nourish her mind, body, and soul, was of great importance to her. Looking and feeling her best was an everyday focus for Gabrielle. As she often said, "I love seeing my outside world reflecting my inside world." Gabrielle truly understood the underlying power of self-appreciation. She fed her soul by helping those in need. Gabrielle was involved at her church soup kitchen. Every Friday afternoon, she helped feed the homeless of Chicago. She also took time to give them the gift of communication. The idea was largely inspired by the stories of her mother helping the *paroissian* in Créteil just before she went to Paris.

Gabrielle loved reading. She always had a book with her. Novels, poetry, and self-help were some of her favorite subjects for nourishing her mind. The sense of being a little different, a little bit more knowledgeable every time she put a book down, inspired her to greatness.

Gabrielle also made time to know and enjoy her body. She had been raised through the French *art de l'amour*, where the concept of shame or shyness about pleasuring your body was non-existent. Every day, she wrote about her fantasies and her future soul mate. She enjoyed describing the romantic scenes and how she would act in them. These moments of self-bliss were her favorite activity before she closed her eyes for the night. Her smile to the angels was a testament to the unity of her mind, body, and soul.

Self-love was no secret to Gabrielle. It was a daily practice that she took pleasure writing about in her journal. She also recounted some of her thoughts with her mother, sometimes to share, other times to seek advice.

One day at teatime, Émilie and Gabrielle sat down to talk about the day ahead. Émilie was wearing a beautiful smile.

"*Maman*, you seem very happy today. Is there something special you want to share?" Gabrielle asked curiously.

"Yes, my angel. Your father and I have been so impressed with your maturity and progress with the principles of self-love that we thought of offering you a little token, a little reminder," said Émilie with joy and excitement in her voice. She reached behind the cushion and took out a silver box with a red bow. "This is for you, sweetheart," Émilie said.

Gabrielle smiled wide. She knew this was going to be very special. She took the box and removed the bow. As she opened the lid she saw exactly what she was hoping for: a magnificent silver ring. Gabrielle gasped.

"Now you have one just like mine. I know that you practice the French *art de l'amour* every day. This will give you additional power," said Émilie.

"Additional power?" repeated Gabrielle.

"Yes, you will see," Émilie added. "Look inside."
Gabrielle looked closely. She saw a simple and powerful engraving, *FA - Self-Love*. She took the ring and put it on the ring finger of her right hand.

"It's beautiful, *Maman*. Thank you so much," Gabrielle said, as she hugged and kissed her mother.

It was the first ring that Gabrielle received on her journey to the French *art de l'amour*. Others would follow.

With inspiration from her new ring, Gabrielle wrote much about self-love over the next several weeks. When she finally finished writing what she had learned about self-love, she turned the page and saw the following passage:

Communion of the soul is about living intimacy in trinity: emotional, physical, and spiritual. It is a gift that can be shared ONLY with the chosen one! Choose carefully... tell me more...

She recognized her mother's writing once more. How did this teaching appear exactly when she was ready to explore and share the principles of intimacy?

Everything happens for a reason.

ஐ*French Secret*ஐ

French Amour: your journal, your destiny, will help guide your steps along this amazing journey that's in front of you.

Gabrielle was only sixteen, but she knew more about intimacy than her friends of the same age. She grew up in the French culture where intimacy principles were talked about openly, without shame or shyness. Gabrielle enjoyed talking to her mother about her feelings regarding *l'amour*. Émilie insisted that in every worthy relationship leading to intimacy there are always three fundamental states: emotional, spiritual, and physical. Gabrielle was familiar with these principles. Although she had never experienced physical intimacy, she had a few romantic friends with whom she felt emotionally intimate.

Gabrielle's journal sat open in front of her that night. She could not write about something she had never experienced before. She could not write about being physically intimate with someone when she had never been. She wanted to keep her journal open to receive this beautiful experience when she was ready to do so. For the moment, she kept this section blank. However, Gabrielle thought of the concept of intimacy from another perspective. She thought that being intimate was not only when you were with someone special, it started with yourself.

A beautiful thought came over her.
Being emotionally intimate with yourself is about being true and honest with your innermost feelings and emotions. It's the courage to bring them to the surface and share them with yourself. My journal is the perfect recipient for these thoughts.

Gabrielle's smile grew. She was proud of her moment of introspection. She continued.

Being physically intimate with myself is when I self-appreciate my body. I take time to explore all of the beautiful sensations. Knowing and taking care of my body by pleasuring it is how I learn about my physical self.

Gabrielle paused for a few seconds. Then her hand started to write almost by itself. It was perhaps another moment of introspection.

Being spiritually intimate is about being connected to God... to His infinite wisdom. In moments of indecision, I ask God for direction. He seems to always guide me along the right path. His eternal love gives me confidence to be who I am and not be afraid to express it.

Gabrielle was impressed with herself. At that moment, she realized that the French *art de l'amour* was really about loving yourself first, being your own very best friend by exhibiting all the traits and characteristics that make you a best friend. It always starts with you being healthy for yourself before being healthy for others entering your life.

Gabrielle's ability to communicate effectively and be empathetic toward others was impeccable. She had that great knowledge from her mother. Émilie had the chance to read, re-read, and explain to Gabrielle the nuances of healthy communication by using the PACT.

Gabrielle made an interesting entry in her journal that night. She had made another discovery. Her journal was a great opportunity for her to reflect and gather her thoughts. She wrote,

The gift of communication is a gift to others. Not many people experience being truly listened to and understood. By proactively focusing on the other person's message, I give them the gift of being understood. Reflecting and summarizing the message shows that I am paying attention. It also helps me understand the message that is being communicated.

The four sins of communication are real. Their use can completely destroy any effort or sense of safety and openness in communication. I have learned this to be true many years ago with Maman. I remember when she took her journal and read to me about Captain John and the way he explained the effects of the four sins. The lesson is clear. I also remember how good I feel when I talk to my mom and dad. Their non-judgmental openness and acceptance encourages me to continue talking to them and open up more.

Gabrielle felt good about her progress and enlightenment into the French *art de l'amour*. She understood and practiced this art every single day.

The fourth and last principle was easy to write about. She had been journaling for so long that she knew her values and goals well. Gabrielle wrote for many days in a row about her dreams and whom she would share her love with. She knew the type of person that would be worthy of her gift. She understood that the better you know who you are and what characterizes you as an individual, the better you will be able to progress in life. Gabrielle was not in a rush to find her true love. She was only sixteen, after all. She wanted to commit to her personal growth and commit to the French *art de l'amour* before she could return the favor to someone she valued. Once again she reminded herself that any healthy relationship started with healthy self-love. It was about growing deep roots into fertile soil where and when the season is right. The fruit of God can only be enjoyed by the best person, the one most worthy of your gift.

❧Gabrielle's Journal☙

Dear Journal,

I am writing to you today not to say goodbye but to greet you.

Where one road ends, another one begins toward the French art de l'amour. *My dear Journal, I have shared so much with you about the fundamental principles of love and happiness these past few years. You know me perfectly now.*

I remember the first day that I wrote to you. I was unsure, without perspective, and immature. I have stayed with you and you helped me discover myself —my true self. I never hid my truth from you, even if it was ugly. You never judged or criticized me. You took me one day at the time, keeping the ground fertile for me to grow from my own reflection.

Today I say to you, "thank you".

You are one of my best friends. Thoughts that were mine are now yours. The fears that were mine are now gone.

The power that you have given me is present every day. Writing to you is writing to myself. Reading about myself gives me perspective. You contain the honest truth of my feelings and thoughts.

My Dear Friend,

It is time to take your first step toward The Four Secret Rings of Love and Happiness.

The seeker seeks their <u>DESTINY</u>.

Your <u>DESTINY</u> will be revealed with <u>CLARITY</u>.

Walk one step at a time on the path to <u>Love and Happiness</u>.

Many times before today, you were reminded that The Four Secret Rings of Love and Happiness starts with yourself.

Givers cannot give back what they do not have in themselves!

Love and happiness starts from the roots of your soul.

Your journal is the soil, your pen is the water, and the sun that makes everything grow is God.

Tell me more…

The Four Secret Rings of Love and Happiness

Conclusion

My Dear Journal...

I was given a gift from above. This gift is now yours. Many tried to take it away, steal it, or bury it with words and actions.

The truth will always prevail.

Faith,

Integrity, and

Kindness

always win over Evil!

The Four Secret Rings of Love and Happiness is my gift to you.

You have probably noticed many changes in your life since you first started to read this book and embraced its philosophy.

The Four Secret Rings of Love and Happiness is quite simple, when you think about it.

However, any simple principle holds a fundamental truth that requires dedication and determination.

Living by the Four Secrets mentioned in this book will transform life around you, starting with your own!

The power that you acquired with this new knowledge is immense.

<u>The Ultimate Secret to incorporate these principles into your daily life is your journal!</u>

Do not underestimate its power!

Your journal is your vessel that will guide you, nourish you, and embrace your new life!

Dedicate time, and it will return your investment a hundred fold.

Your daily introspection will bring you many breakthroughs.

Your focus on incorporating The Four Secret Rings of Love and Happiness into your life will be supported by your precious journal.

Merci!

Richard Henry II Hains

Join our private Facebook *group*
French Amour Elite Club

Our Elite Club comes with great privileges.

Not only will you be joining like-minded friends who focus on love and happiness, but you will benefit from amazing savings on our upcoming products.

www.ingramcontent.com/pod-product-compliance
Lightning Source LLC
LaVergne TN
LVHW041541070426
835507LV00011B/865